LIORoooosh

Baking from My Tel Aviv Kitchen

Lior Mashiach

LIOROOOOSH

Baking from My Tel Aviv Kitchen

Lior Mashiach

Editor | **Anna O. Aleksandrowicz**
Gastronomic Editor | **Nomi Abeliovich**
Photographer | **Michal Revivo**
Styling | **Galia Ornan**
Designer | **Studio Keren & Golan**
Proofreader | **Karen Marron**
Printed by | **Regent Publishing Services**

Baking dishes by **Adi Nissani**

Photos on pages 214, 215, 229: provided courtesy of **Dror Einav**
Photos on pages 24, 25, 32, 106, 240, 243: by **Lior Mashiach**

Second Edition in English: 2023

LunchBox Press
Publisher and Editor-in-Chief | **Ofer Vardi**
www.lunch-box.co.il / info@lunch-box.co.il
www.facebook.com/LunchBoxPress

Printed in China 2023
ISBN: 9781602804302

TABLE OF CONTENTS

RECIPES

BAKING CONVERSION GUIDE

This guide will help you to convert amounts and weights in this book into your preferred scale, so that you don't have to look up the differences between grams, cups, etc.

Before you start baking, I recommend that you buy a kitchen scale. A battery-operated kitchen scale will make your life so much easier in the kitchen, and once you have it, you'll wonder how you ever lived without one! Also, if you like to use cups and spoons rather than weights, I really encourage you to invest in a set of professional measuring spoons and cups.

Measurements

1 teaspoon	5 ml			
1 tablespoon	15 ml			
1 fluid oz	30 ml			
2 fluid oz	60 ml	1/4 cup		
	80 ml	1/3 cup		
	100 ml	1/3 cup + 1 Tbs		
4 fluid oz	120 ml	1/2 cup		
6 fluid oz	180 ml	3/4 cup		
8 fluid oz	240 ml	1 cup		
16 fluid oz	475 ml	2 cups	1 pint	
	950 ml	4 cups	2 pints	1 quart
	3.8 L	4 quarts		1 gallon

Good to Know

1 tablespoon	3 teaspoons	
4 tablespoons	1/4 cup	
1 ounce	28 grams	
1 pound	16 ounces	450 grams
1 cup self-rising flour	1 cup all-purpose flour + 1 tsp baking powder	
1 gram active dry yeast	3 grams fresh yeast	

Butter Measurements

1 tablespoon			0.5 oz	14 grams
4 tablespoons	½ stick		2 oz	57 grams
8 tablespoons	1 stick	½ cup	4 oz	113 grams
16 tablespoons	2 sticks	1 cup	8 oz	227 grams

Oven Baking Temperatures

This table lists the temperatures to use with your oven, depending on the type of oven you have—Fahrenheit, Celsius, or gas. My oven also has a settings button (as do many ovens today), so when baking, I use the turbo setting, which looks like this:

Fahrenheit	*Celsius*	*Gas Mark*
225 °F	110 °C	¼
250 °F	130 °C	½
275 °F	140 °C	1
300 °F	150 °C	2
325 °F	165 °C	3
350 °F	177 °C	4
375 °F	190 °C	5
400 °F	200 °C	6
425 °F	220 °C	7
450 °F	230 °C	8
475 °F	245 °C	9

INTRODUCTION

“How old did you say you were?” That's the question I'm asked most often after my introduction spiel at every workshop, brunch, or event I host. Maybe it’s the babyface, or maybe it’s the fact that in the space of a few years, I’ve worked and interned at some of the best restaurants in the world.

So here it is: I’m Lior Mashiach, and I was born in 1987 in a small town outside of Tel Aviv, Israel. I'm an internationally-trained pastry chef based in Tel Aviv, and my business is called Lioroooosh, as is my social media persona. My path down "Pastry Lane" began a long time ago, and started with my food-loving family.

My mom, Yael, loved spending time in the kitchen, even while running an insurance business, and both of my grandmothers, Savta Victoria (Vicki) and Savta Rivka (Pika), were exquisite cooks. So it's no surprise that my brothers (Amit and Yoav) and I inherited that love of the kitchen, and even though I'm the chef in the family, both my brothers also love to cook.

I began my love affair with the kitchen when I was little: At a very young age, I used to come up to my mom as she was cooking or baking and ask if I could help. I still remember standing on a stool as a little girl, mixing cake batter with a wooden spoon, and then licking the leftovers in the mixing bowl. It was only later in life that I was surprised to learn that not everyone cooks, and more importantly, that not every person enjoys cooking! But in our house, there was always good food to eat; I remember on weekends, my mom would cook mountains of food to make sure we had a warm, home-cooked lunch every day after school, even though she was working all day. For me, my mom is the best role model in the world: She's a Wonder Woman and a ninja who just makes it all look so easy!

Before moving to New York to study the art of pastry, I worked for several years in informal education programs at youth movements, teaching kids and teenagers, which I absolutely loved, but at some point I felt I like should be doing something else. While I felt comfortable stepping into the kitchen from a very young age, at that point, still in my early twenties, I hadn't yet baked professionally, although I'd wanted to. I thought I'd begin by studying the art of pastry making and take it from there, to see where that path led me. My family, with my mom leading the charge, encouraged me (let's be honest–pressured me) to study abroad. At that point there were few pastry schools in Israel, and the level of training they provided wasn't that great. My mom wanted me to study in France, which really appealed to me, so I began my research into finding the best pastry school in the world.

My research eventually led me to the French Culinary Institute (FCI) in New York, which became the International Culinary Center (ICC) and, more recently, a part of the Institute of Culinary Education (ICE). But before I began my studies, I thought it would make sense to gain some experience in a restaurant kitchen. I began working at a restaurant called Raphael in Tel Aviv. Raphael has closed since then, but back in the day, it was truly one of the best restaurants in town. Working at Raphael was one of the best decisions I've ever made; Raphael helped me to gain an understanding of working in a professional, high-end kitchen. This meant consistency, preparing every dish precisely like the previous one, and working at the highest standards. Oh, and also CLEANLINESS! Oh, yes! Raphael is where I learned just how important it is to work in a clean environment all the time, since we would clean the kitchen three times a day! Before working at Raphael, that need for absolute cleanliness wasn't that obvious to me, but today it's an inseparable aspect of my work.

At Raphael, I also learned how to fully take advantage of one my best qualities:

I'm really fast. I think fast, I move fast, I work fast. That's quite an advantage when working in a kitchen, and that quality would serve me well in my studies. My peers used to call me "overachiever," and we'd joke that their goal in our exams was to finish before me. In addition, by the time I started my studies, I knew what it was like to work in a professional kitchen, a decision that served me well.

I spent almost two years in Manhattan, during which time I interned everywhere I could. My first internship in the city was at Chef Mario Batali's Eataly, in the fresh pasta station. At Eataly, the pasta station is an aquarium where you can see the chefs preparing the fresh pasta right in front of you. So it wasn't your typical pastry internship, but I wanted to learn how to make professional handmade pasta, and let me tell you—that was definitely the best place to learn. My second internship was at the Mercer Kitchen in Soho. I worked in the pastry department there, and that felt closer to home, since the work I was doing at the Mercer Kitchen was quite similar to the work I did in Tel Aviv at Raphael.

The third and last internship I had in New York was completely different from the previous two. First of all, it was full-time—Monday to Friday, morning until afternoon—and it was all about cakes, RBI Cakes to be precise! (RBI Cakes is the cake studio of celebrity chef and cake designer Ron Ben-Israel.) During my studies, my chefs had pointed out that I had an instinct for decorated cakes, something that at the time was not at all a "thing" in Israel, so I had no idea I'd be good at it. They encouraged me to apply for an internship at Ron Ben-Israel's wedding cake studio, and I was lucky enough to get in. Over the next four months, I made sugar flowers, baked, and built beautiful cakes, and learned all about the "art of the small details." It was an amazing experience, and so different from working in a restaurant.

I completed my studies and returned to Israel, but it wasn't easy to figure out my next step. I knew a lot of people in the restaurant industry, but so much had changed in nearly two years; new places had opened, and I was lucky to get job offers from so many of them. I finally started working at Pronto in Tel Aviv, one of my favorite Italian restaurants in town, which had just hired a new young chef who was looking to make things interesting. Boy, was that a smart choice! David Frenkel, my chef, wasn't afraid of pastry like so many other chefs I knew, so working with him meant I was actually working *with* him.

David was an active part of the creative process: He had great ideas, he knew all sorts of cool new techniques, and he was, and still is, a full-on artist. Which is, I guess, why he was so supportive when I gave him the news: I'd just been accepted to intern in the best restaurant in the world. In the summer of 2015, I flew to Copenhagen for four months to intern at Noma. I was very lucky to have a supportive chef, who had also interned there a few years before, and remembered how important it was to make sure that his staff continued to learn and grow.

GOOD PEOPLE AGE

When I started my internship at Noma, I decided to write a blog about my experience. I suppose it was mostly for my own benefit, so that I could process my time there and the things I learned, and also to have something I could go back to and read, a journal of my experience that would help me to appreciate my time at Noma. I would sit down every week on my day off, and write about the previous week: at which station I'd worked, what we did, how it went—everything.

I shared the blog with my friends, and they shared it with their friends, and it wasn't long before people I didn't know started reading my blog. Now, while I was growing up, I used to write, but when I started working in restaurants, I kind of stopped doing that. I'm not sure why, maybe because I didn't have the time, maybe because it wasn't the right moment, but the months I spent at Noma made me remember that I loved writing. So when I came back to Israel, I tried to keep my blog going. It was hard at first, because what was I going to write about now? How was I going to keep the blog interesting? About a year later, I started writing a weekly column for a local online magazine called *Walla Food*, and to this day I write for a different magazine, called *Hashulchan*. I also found my "blog voice" again, and am proud to say that I continue to write my blog on a regular basis, mostly recipes these days.

But, let's go back to 2015. The experience at Noma was incredible. What a rollercoaster ride! Today I feel that I truly appreciate just how much I actually did there, how much I learned, how many friends I made, friends I'm still in touch with to this day. But back then, in the moment, its wasn't always easy to see beyond the day-to-day. After all, this was the best restaurant in the world, and I was trying to prove myself and survive. And somehow, I actually did!

When I came back to Israel and to Pronto, there was a lot of excitement, and a lot of expectation from the people around me, including from my chef and from me, to apply the methods, the techniques, and the flavors that I had learned about and used in Noma, at the restaurant. So I tried. And boy, did I fail. That year, I failed more than I ever had until that point. Something just wasn't working for me, and I felt like I'd lost my *mojo*.

A year after I returned from Noma, I decided to take a few months off to travel, to recharge, to find new inspirations, and to taste new flavors. I travelled to Japan; I spent a few life-changing months in Australia with my brother Yoav; and finally I spent some time in Thailand. When I returned to Israel, I wasn't sure what I was going to do next. I decided to build a baking studio where I could host workshops; in retrospect, I think I really wanted my own place, to start my own business. What I didn't realize at the time was that this studio would also become my home and the heart of my business. I wanted to have a setting—and a platform—where I could teach others, where I could pass on my knowledge and the techniques behind pastry making, making this very special field accessible. Within a short time, my workshop studio had also become a tiny restaurant, where I hosted people for meals, and a place where people would come to buy special baked goods and pastries; last summer I even started taking groups on culinary market tours, in the beautiful Lewinski Market in my neighborhood. Thus, this studio, my home, has become one of the best business decisions I've ever made.

I recently realized just how much of an influence Noma has had on me; I now understand that some experiences, especially the life-changing ones, take time to sink in. Some of you might think that because Noma is a Michelin-starred restaurant, it must be stuck up, snobbish. But you couldn't be more wrong! Noma is **the** place, the one place I know, that will always accept you as you are, no matter what you wear, no matter where you come from. When you step through the door, every single person—including the chefs, the wait staff, and even the dish washer—will all stop everything they're doing, and come to the front of the house to welcome you. And from that moment on, you feel like you're the most important person in the world. And you feel like you've come home.

And that's what I feel I've learned from Noma. In addition to gaining a whole new respect for the ingredients that go into our cooking, I've learned what it truly means to be a host. Anyone can host people, but not everyone is a **host**. When people step through my door, to my actual home, which is where my studio is, I want them to feel like they're the most important people in the world. Like they're my VIPs, regardless of who they are.

So, why am I writing this book and who is it for?

Everyone.

When I started hosting baking workshops, my goal was to make professional baking accessible to all, at least to everyone who wanted to learn baking. In the past few years, I've been teaching people how to make simple, yet unique, dishes and pastries, and that's the same goal for me in this book. Now, some of the recipes in this book are super simple, and some are a little more challenging, but they're all my top, my best recipes, my favorite ones, and they're all delicious, special, and absolutely worth the effort.

So, whether you bake professionally, or whether baking is a hobby, or even if you're terrified of baking—this book is for all of you. Nearly all of the recipes in this book have a story behind them, because, just in case you haven't noticed yet, I'm not only a baker, but a storyteller. So either way, I hope you enjoy the ride.

Thank you for believing in me.
Lior

Section 1

It's Not Shabbat Without Challah

#shabbatchallah

Challah is a loaf of white, leavened bread, typically braided, which is baked to celebrate the Jewish Sabbath (Shabbat). Traditionally, you'd bake the challah on a Friday, and then it would be blessed and eaten as part of the Friday evening meal and also on Saturday morning. Challah became an important–indeed central–part of my life long before I realized it. I didn't really bake challah very much before I started working at restaurants, and to be honest, I don't think I even baked it for fun.

When I started my first professional position as a pastry cook at Raphael (which used to be a famous restaurant in Tel Aviv), every Friday and every Saturday (Shabbat) I would bake, in addition to the regular bread and Raphael's famous focaccia, challah for the service. These were challahs made from a rich dough that included butter—"almost brioche," Raphael's chef, Rafi Cohen, called it, and that was true (challah is usually made without butter, to ensure that it's parve, meaning non-dairy). This challah was something between a classic challah and brioche.

At Raphael, the emphasis was on precision at the highest levels, so the challahs had to be identical and consistent. Because every challah had to weigh exactly the same, I'd roll the leftover dough into a large bun and bake it as a treat for the staff. Not the entire staff, mind you, because there were a lot of people, just for the cooks, because the cooks who worked on the weekend were missing their family meals. Making this bun was my way of giving them and myself a little fringe benefit: challah, once a week.

I continued this same tradition years later, while working as a pastry chef at Pronto (another famous Tel Aviv restaurant). At Pronto, challah wasn't a part of the menu, so I didn't prepare it on a regular basis. Instead, whenever I could, I would make a point of making challah for the entire staff on Saturday. (In Israel, Saturday is our day off, not Sunday; however, in the restaurant business, you work *every day*.) While the cooks would make a large shakshuka (poached eggs cooked in a sauce made of tomatoes, olive oil, and garlic and seasoned with spices, that's usually served at breakfast)—I would add my delicious challah, and we'd have this extra bonus for all the "little soldiers" working on a Saturday. That made our Saturday meal together into a ceremony—in fact, into a family get-together. Why else do you think they call staff meals at restaurants a "family meal"? What could be more natural than eating a Saturday morning meal with my work family?

That's when I began posting a picture on Instagram every Saturday of my weekly challah with the hashtag in Hebrew "it's not Shabbat without challah," a tradition that continues to this day.

CLASSIC CHALLAH

Below you'll see an example of a braided challah prepared according to this recipe; with the exception of the shape, all the instructions remain the same when you choose to braid instead of baking in a pan.

Makes two 5-strand braided challahs

-

For the dough

½ cup + 2 tsp (130 ml) lukewarm water

3 tsp (12 grams) active dry yeast

4 cups (550 grams) all-purpose flour or bread flour

⅓ cup (75 grams) sugar

2 tsp (12 grams) salt

2 eggs

3 egg yolks

¼ cup (60 ml) extra virgin olive oil

-

For the topping

1 beaten egg, for brushing

nigella seeds, poppy seeds, sesame seeds, or any other topping of your choice

1. Place the water, yeast, flour, sugar, salt, eggs, and yolks in the bowl of a stand mixer fitted with the dough hook. Mix on a low speed (1) until the dough comes together. Increase the speed slightly (to 2) and knead for 7 minutes, until you have a soft, smooth dough.

2. Add the olive oil in 4 phases, while continuously kneading, each time pouring it in a slow, steady stream. Knead until the oil is fully incorporated into the dough. Do not be afraid to over-knead.

3. Transfer the dough to a greased bowl, shape into a ball, cover with a towel or a loose plastic wrap, and let rise for 30 minutes, until it doubles in volume.

4. Punch down the dough, cover, and let rise for another 30 minutes.

5. Place the dough on a clean surface and divide it into 10 equal balls, about 3.5 oz (100 grams) each. Roll each ball into a strand, 35–40 cm (13–15 in) long; I like my strands plumper in the center and thinner on the ends. Cover and let rest for 10 minutes.

6. Roll the strands and braid the challahs (*see image on page 30*).

7. Transfer the challahs to a baking tray lined with parchment paper and brush with a thin coat of beaten egg. Cover with a towel or a loose plastic wrap and let rise at room temperature for 1 hour.

8. Preheat the oven to 180 °C (350 °F).

9. Brush the challah with the beaten egg a second time and sprinkle the seeds.

10. Bake for 20–25 minutes, until the challah is a deep, even shade of golden brown. Cool on a rack.

5-strand braid
(for instructions see page 30)

5-strand braid
(for instructions see page 30)

Braiding Time!

For me, the fun part of baking challah is the braiding. That's where you can really go crazy! Create different shapes, different sizes, connect the shape of the challah to the theme of the meal, or maybe even add different ingredients to it. There are literally thousands of challah braiding techniques worldwide; which one you choose is a question of your mood and preferences.

Since I love braiding challah, it seems natural to me to take you on a braiding journey, and I've decided to show you a few of my favorite braiding techniques.

2-STRAND CHALLAH

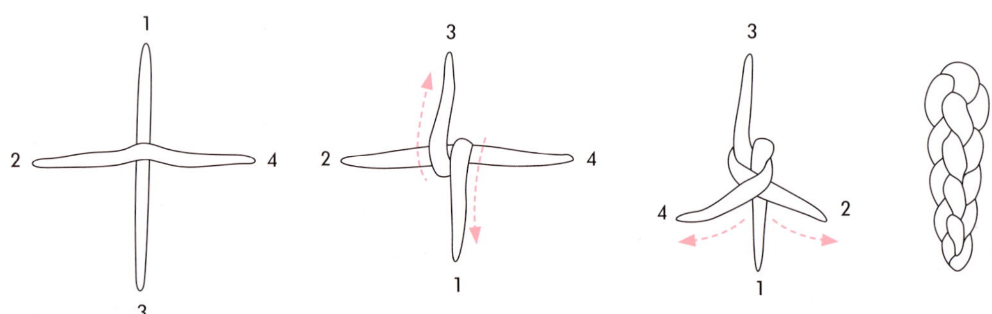

4-STRAND CHALLAH

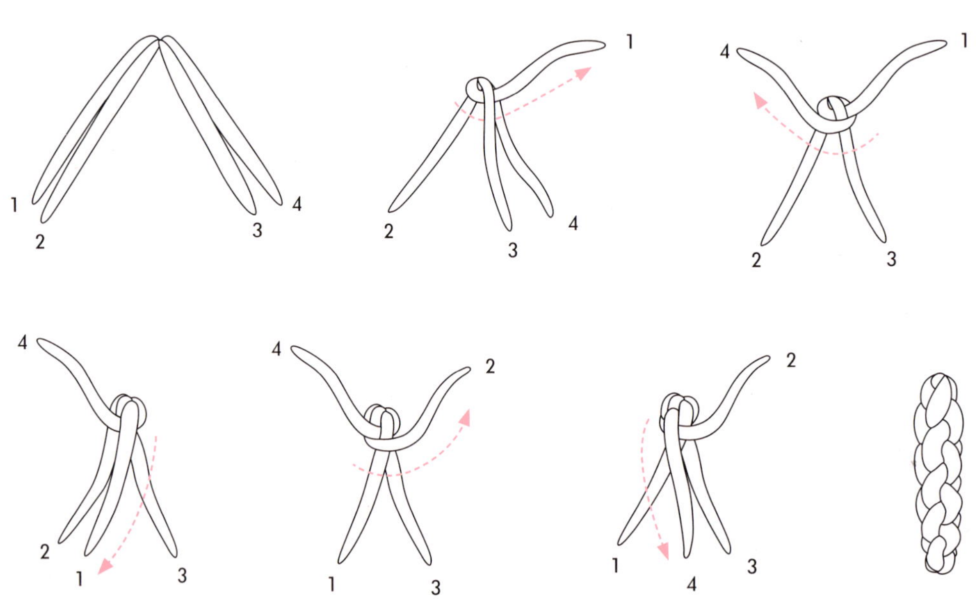

5-STRAND CHALLAH

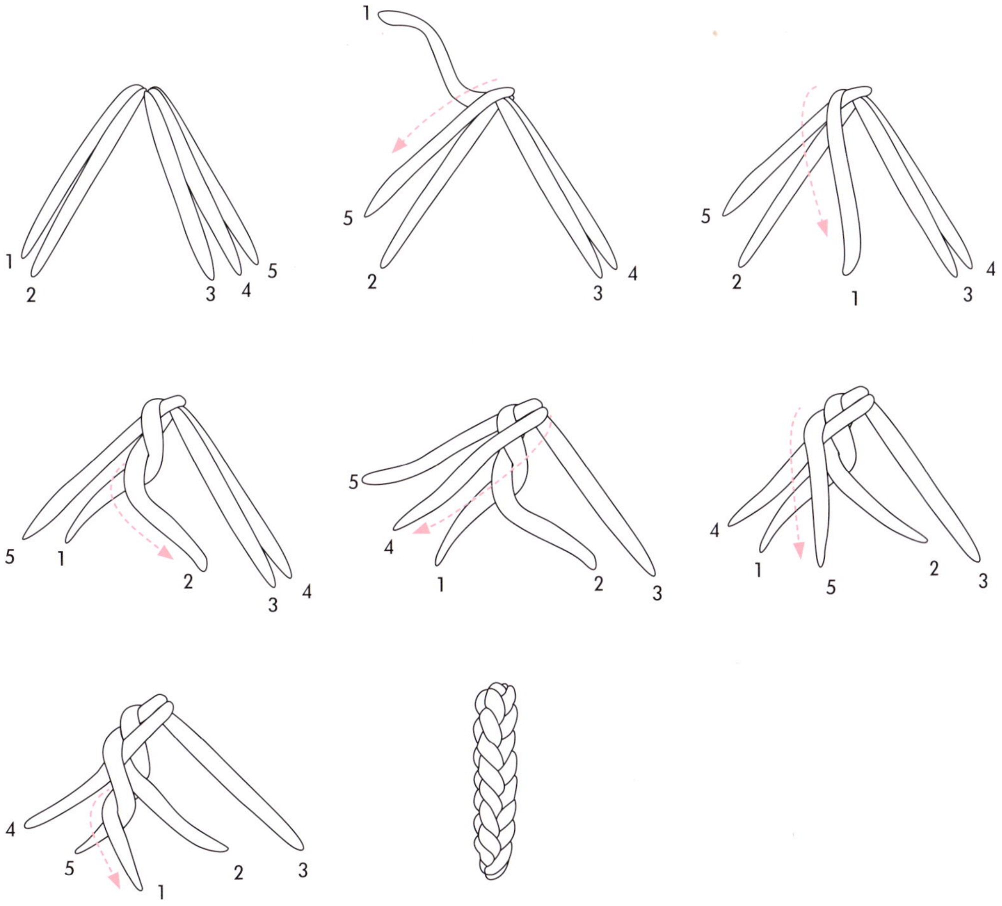

6-STRAND CHALLAH

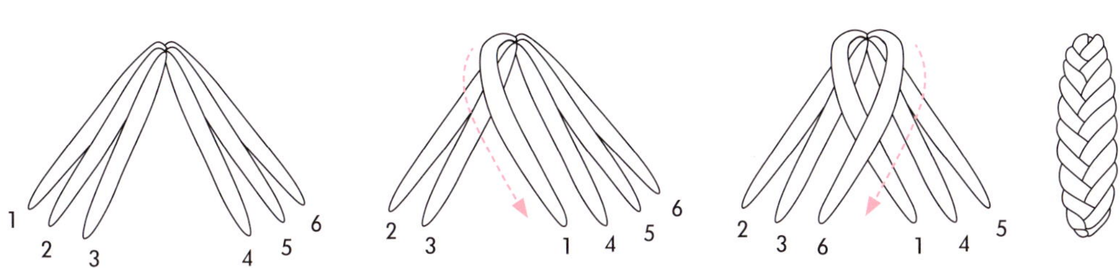

4-strand round braid
(for instructions see page 29)

BEETROOT CHALLAH

For a beetroot challah, use the Classic Challah recipe (*see page* 22), but replace the water with:
½ cup (110 grams) beetroot puree
(see explanation below)
or
100 ml water + 2 Tbs beetroot powder
(available online and in specialty shops).

Beetroot Puree

1. Preheat the oven to 180–200 °C (355–390 °F). Wrap a large beetroot in foil and roast until it's soft.

2. Remove from the oven and peel.

3. Place the beetroot in a food processor, add 2–3 tablespoons of water, and process into a smooth puree.

4. Cool the puree to room temperature before adding it to the batter.

ZA'ATAR (HYSSOP) AND SUMAC CHALLAH

Add **2 Tbs dried za'atar** (hyssop) and **3 Tbs sumac** (both available online and in Mediterranean spice shops) to step 1 in the Classic Challah *(see recipe on page 22)* or Brioche Challah dough (*see recipe on page* 92).

4-STRAND CHALLAH - *round*

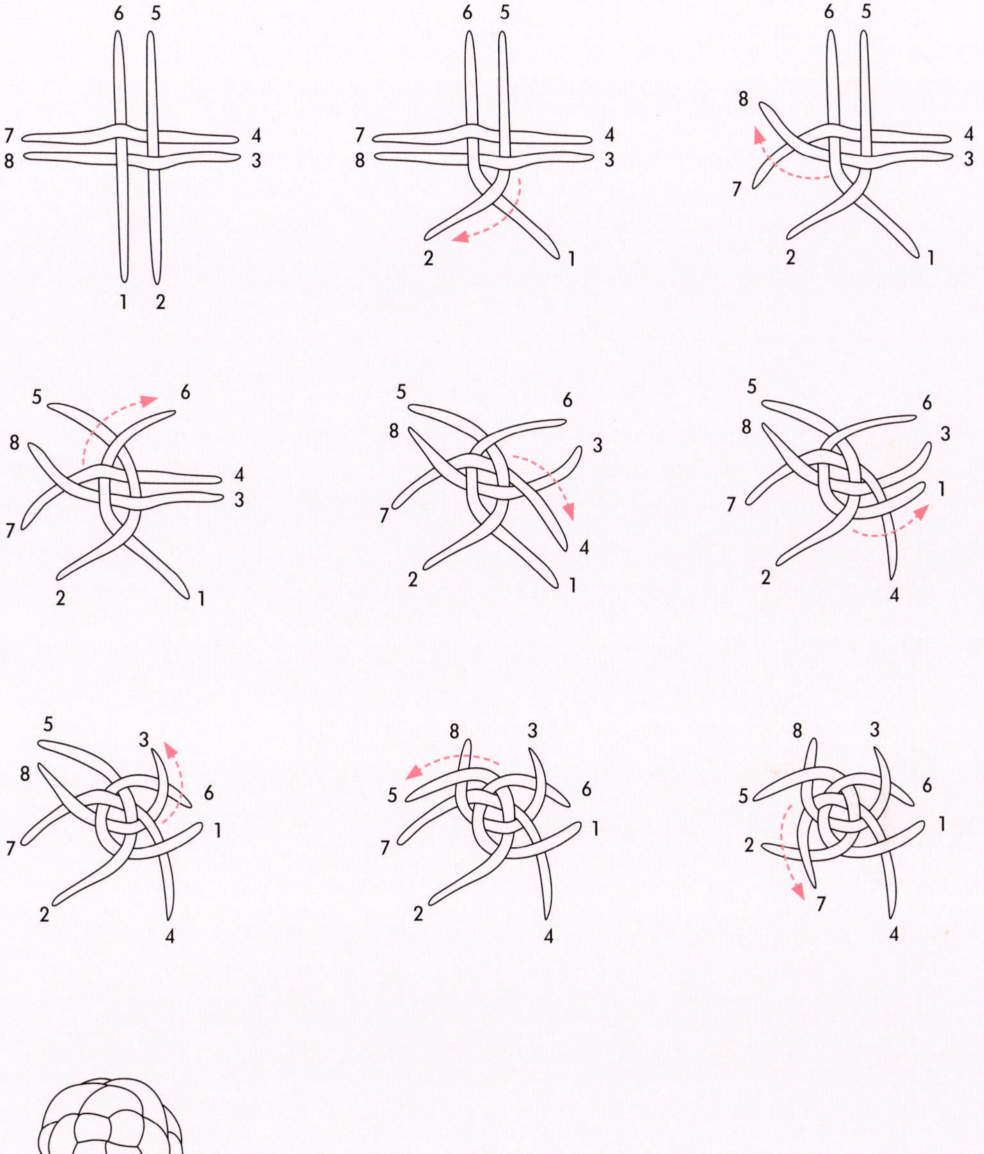

4-strand braid
(for instructions see page 29)

6-strand braid (for instructions see page 30)

MATCHA AND BLACK SESAME CHALLAH

Add **4 Tbs matcha green tea powder** to step 1 in the classic challah (*see recipe on page 22*). After brushing with a beaten egg in step 9, sprinkle the challah with **black sesame seeds**.

BLACK AND WHITE CHALLAH

To end up with a black and white challah, you'll need to prepare two doughs.

Makes two 5-strand braided challahs

-

For the white dough

¼ cup + 1 tsp (65 ml) lukewarm water

1 ½ tsp (6 grams) active dry yeast

2 cups (275 grams) all-purpose flour or bread flour

3 ½ Tbs (40 grams) sugar

1 tsp (6 grams) salt

2 eggs

1 egg yolk

2 Tbs (30 ml) extra virgin olive oil

-

For the black dough

¼ cup + 1 tsp (65 grams) lukewarm water

1 ½ tsp (6 grams) active dry yeast

2 cups (275 grams) all-purpose flour or bread flour

1 Tbs (10 grams) activated charcoal powder (available online and in specialty shops)

3 ½ Tbs (40 grams) sugar

1 tsp (6 grams) salt

2 eggs

1 egg yolk

2 Tbs (30 ml) extra virgin olive oil

1. Prepare the white dough according to steps 1-4 of the classic challah recipe (*see recipe on page* 22).

2. Prepare the black dough according to steps 1-4 of the classic challah recipe (*see recipe on page* 22), adding the charcoal powder to the dough mixture in step 1 of the classic challah dough to create the black dough.

3. Follow steps 5 and on in the classic challah recipe (*page* 22) to prepare the challahs using the black and white doughs. Divide each dough into 5 equal balls, about 3.5 oz (100 grams) each.

4-strand braid (for instructions see page 29)

Uri, my significant other, gets to enjoy everything I make—including any experiment I undertake (as you can see from the story of my Kremugit recipe on page 241). Last Valentine's Day, Uri decided to surprise me (I love surprises), and as luck would have it, I was out of the house all day, so he took over my kitchen and decided to make me a beautiful Valentine's Day meal. His original plan was to make an entire meal based on my recipes, but that proved too much (Uri is also an overachiever), and in the end he made me sushi and then baked me a pumpkin challah with spelt flour.

Because Uri is not a baker, he didn't realize that the white flour called for in the recipe should not be self-rising flour. But the challah turned out pretty nice nonetheless, and, most importantly, it was a wonderful gesture on his part, and I was truly moved. It's also a good reminder that unless a recipe specifically calls for self-rising flour, use only regular white flour and the end result will be perfect.

Traditionally, challah isn't sliced but pulled-apart. Pull-apart bread is usually baked in a rectangular pan, such as an English cake pan or a loaf pan, but I bake my pumpkin challah in a terrine dish. Baking in a ceramic dish also has the advantage of spreading the heat evenly throughout the pan, which is nice. But that doesn't mean you can't bake challah in a stainless-steel English cake pan.

This pull-apart challah can be baked in a loaf pan or shaped into a free-form braided challah.

PUMPKIN CHALLAH WITH SPELT FLOUR

Makes 1 pull-apart challah

-

For the dough

75 grams (2.6 oz) roasted pumpkin (see recipe below)

1 tsp (4 grams) active dry yeast

1 egg yolk

2 Tbs (25 grams) sugar

½ tsp (4 grams) salt

1 cup (125 grams) whole meal spelt flour

¾ cup+ 2 Tbs (125 grams) all-purpose flour

⅓ cup (80 ml) water

1 ½ Tbs (20 ml) extra virgin olive oil

-

For the roasted pumpkin

100 grams (3.5 oz) pumpkin

1-2 Tbs extra virgin olive oil

A pinch of salt

-

For the topping

1 beaten egg, for brushing

A mix of your favorite seeds (pumpkin, sunflower, sesame, poppy seeds)

1. **To prepare the pumpkin:** Preheat the oven to 180 °C (350 °F) and line a baking tray with parchment paper. Peel the pumpkin and remove the seeds. Cut the pumpkin coarsely into large, even chunks. Drizzle with olive oil, season with a little salt, and roast until soft. Let cool.

2. **To prepare the dough:** Place the roasted pumpkin, yeast, eggs, sugar, salt, and flours in the bowl of a stand mixer fitted with the dough hook. Mix on a low speed until the dough comes together.

3. Pour the water slowly and while continuously mixing, just until the dough comes together. You may not need to use all of the water. Increase the speed slightly and knead for 10 minutes, until you have a soft, smooth dough.

4. Reduce to a low speed. Add the olive oil in 4 phases, kneading continuously, each time pouring it in a slow, steady stream. Knead until the oil is fully incorporated. Do not be afraid to over-knead.

5. Transfer the dough to a greased bowl, shape into a ball, cover with a towel, and let rise 45 minutes.

6. Place the dough on a clean worksurface and split into 4 equal pieces. Roll each piece into a ball, cover, and let rest 5-10 minutes.

7. Grease the loaf pan and line with parchment paper. Roll the dough balls and place in the pan. Brush a thin coat of the beaten egg, cover with a towel, and let rise at room temperature for 1 hour.

8. Preheat the oven to 180 °C (350 °F). Brush the loaf with the beaten egg and sprinkle the seeds. Bake 25-30 minutes, until the challah is a deep, even shade of golden brown. Cool on a rack before pulling it apart.

Egg Salad
(page 57)
Quinoa Salad
(page 57)
Butternut Squash
Bread Roll
(page 82)
Potato Bread Roll
(page 85)

Section 2

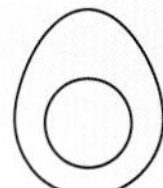

Breakfasts and Brunches

Weekends Are Made for Breakfast

I'm a big fan of repurposing leftovers from the previous night, and making them into something (ideally into breakfast). One of the easiest options is French toast, which you can make from pretty much anything baked: babka, challah, or even flaky brioche—just use your imagination. But when it comes to breakfast or brunch for a weekend or Saturday breakfast, I love to get creative with my recipes, choosing both sweet and savory combinations that should satisfy the most demanding palate.

Early on in the COVID-19 pandemic, when Israel was on lockdown, *The Nosher*, a Jewish food website, hosted me for a live Facebook event on how make kubaneh. The host asked me about the origin of this bread, where it came from, and how I'd begun making it. I explained that while I'm not from a Yemenite background, I love making this traditional breakfast bread, which also goes well with additions like cheese, brown-butter, chocolate—the sky's the limit.

A local Yemenite recipe, kubaneh was adapted by the Yemenite Jews to meet their economic and observance needs. The kubaneh was perfect for the Yemenite Jewish community both because of its low cost and because it can be cooked slowly, overnight, for the Sabbath morning meal.

In Yemen, each family would prepare their kubaneh before Shabbat; they would prepare the dough with a lot of *samneh*, smoked clarified butter, because the kubaneh is supposed to be very festive. Then, they would shape the dough into a beautiful shape and take it to the regional oven, where it would bake overnight. Each family would then pick up its own baked kubaneh and place it in the center of their Shabbat table. Because the kubaneh is shaped liked a crown, it added a wonderful, festive, decorative feeling to the Shabbat table.

Why a crown? The point of the kubaneh is to be a symbolic, festive bread, something that's more special and beautiful than an everyday loaf of bread, so while I didn't grow up with this bread on my table, it's a natural fit for me as a pastry chef. There are also a lot of different ways to shape kubaneh, and that's another one of the things that I love–the shaping. When you turn the kubaneh over, it looks like a bouquet of flowers, and nothing to me says "it's Shabbat" more than a fresh bouquet of flowers.

KUBANEH (YEMENITE JEWISH PULL-APART BREAD)

You'll need a large kubaneh pan or a wonder pot (however, kubaneh also works with a regular round cake pan).

Makes 1 kubaneh baked in a kubaneh pan or 20-cm (8-in) round cake pan

-

½ cup + 2 tsp (130 ml) water

2 tsp (8 grams) instant dry yeast

2 eggs

3 egg yolks

4 cups (550 grams) all-purpose flour

¼ cup + 2 Tbs (75 grams) sugar

2 tsp (12 grams) salt

½ cup (120 ml) extra virgin olive oil

14 Tbs (200 grams) butter, at room temperature, for greasing the pan and shaping the dough

1. Place the water, yeast, eggs, egg yolks, flour, sugar, and salt in the bowl of a stand mixer fitted with the dough hook, and mix on a low speed for about 1 minute, until dough forms.

2. Increase the speed to medium low and knead for 5–7 minutes to a smooth, soft dough. Add the olive oil and knead until it's fully incorporated into the dough. Do not be afraid to over-knead.

3. Shape the dough into a ball and place in a greased bowl. Cover with a towel or a loose plastic wrap and let rise for 30 minutes at room temperature. Don't worry if the dough hasn't risen much.

4. Punch down the dough, cover, and let rise for another 30 minutes.

5. Grease the kubaneh pan or cake pan thoroughly and generously with butter.

6. Divide the dough into 8 equal pieces, roll into balls, and place on a greased plate. Brush the dough balls with butter and cover loosely with a plastic wrap. Let rest for 10 minutes.

7. Grease your hands and the worksurface with a spoonful of butter. Using your hands, press, flatten, and stretch a dough ball into a large square as thin as you possibly can, without tearing it.

8. Fold the sides of the dough toward the center, and then roll from the bottom to the top into a cylinder shape. Repeat this with the remaining dough balls.

→

9. Using a sharp knife, cut each cylinder in half, into 2 smaller cylinders, and place in an even layer in the kubaneh pan, cut side facing up. Continue until the pan is full and you've used all the dough.

10. Brush some butter on top of the unbaked kubaneh, cover, and let rise at room temperature for about 1 hour.

11. Preheat the oven to 100 °C (220 °F).

12. Cover the kubaneh with aluminum foil, making sure to leave the top loose to allow the dough to rise while baking.

13. Bake for 8–10 hours. Every 2 hours or so, brush the kubaneh with 1–2 tablespoons of butter.

14. Release the kubaneh from the pan and place on a cooling rack.

BROWN-BUTTER KUBANEH

Substitute the butter in the recipe above with **brown-butter**, cooled to room temperature. Optional: You can also add **2 cups (300 grams) chopped Gianduja chocolate** and sprinkle **a tablespoon of chopped chocolate** on each dough rectangle before folding and rolling into cylinders.

Makes 1 kubaneh baked in a kubaneh pan or 20-cm (8-in) round cake pan

Brown-Butter

1. Melt 1 cup (230 grams) butter in a small pot over medium heat.

2. As the butter melts it will begin to foam and gradually turn a toasty brown color and release a nutty aroma.

3. Remove from the heat and transfer to a bowl to cool.

CASHEW, BLUE CHEESE, AND ARTICHOKE KUBANEH

Makes 1 kubaneh baked in a kubaneh pan or 20-cm (8-in) round cake pan

-

For the dough

- 1/2 cup (110 ml) water
- 2 tsp (8 grams) instant dry yeast
- 2 eggs
- 3 egg yolks
- 4 cups (550 grams) all-purpose flour
- 1/4 cup + 2 Tbs (75 grams) sugar
- 2 tsp (12 grams) salt
- 1/2 cup (120 ml) extra virgin olive oil
- 2/3 cup (150 grams) butter, at room temperature, for greasing the pan and shaping the dough

-

For the filling

- 1 cup (150 grams) cashew nuts, coarsely chopped
- 7 oz (200 grams) Gorgonzola or any other blue cheese, crumbled
- 10.5 oz (300 grams) jarred, grilled artichokes in olive oil, strained and chopped or quartered

1. Place the water, yeast, eggs, egg yolks, flour, sugar, and salt in the bowl of a stand mixer fitted with the dough hook and mix on a low speed for about 1 minute, until dough forms.

2. Increase the speed to medium low and knead for 5–7 minutes to a smooth, soft dough. Add the olive oil and knead until it's fully incorporated into the dough. Do not be afraid to over-knead.

3. Shape the dough into a ball and place in a greased bowl. Cover with a towel or a loose plastic wrap and let rise for 30 minutes at room temperature. Don't worry if the dough hasn't risen much.

4. Punch down the dough, cover, and let rise for another 30 minutes.

5. Grease the kubaneh pan or cake pan thoroughly and generously with butter

6. Divide the dough into 8 equal pieces, roll into balls, and place on a greased plate. Brush the dough balls with butter and cover loosely with a plastic wrap. Let rest for 10 minutes.

7. Grease your hands and the worksurface with a spoonful of butter. Using your hands, press, flatten, and stretch a dough ball to a large rectangle, as thin as you possibly can, without tearing it.

8. Place 3-5 pieces of artichoke, 1 1/2 tablespoons of crumbled Gorgonzola cheese, and 7–10 cashew nuts in the center of the rectangle. Fold the sides toward the center, and then roll from the bottom to the top into a cylinder shape. Repeat this with the remaining dough balls.

→

9. Using a sharp knife, cut each cylinder in half, into 2 smaller cylinders, and place in an even layer in the kubaneh pan, cut side facing up. Continue until the pan is full and you've used all the dough.

10. Brush some butter on top of the unbaked kubaneh, cover, and let rise at room temperature for about 40 minutes.

11. Preheat the oven to 180 °C (350 °F).

12. Bake for 15 minutes. reduce the oven temperature to 160 °C (320 °F) and bake for 30–40 minutes, until the kubaneh is a deep golden brown.

13. Release the kubaneh from the pan and place on a cooling rack.

CINNAROLL KUBANEH

Kubaneh is a pastry that's baked overnight on a low temperature or on 180 °C (350 °F) for between 40 to 60 minutes

Makes 1 kubaneh baked in a kubaneh pan or 20-cm (8-in) round cake pan

–

For the dough

½ cup (110 ml) water

2 tsp (8 grams) instant dry yeast

2 eggs

3 egg yolks

4 cups (550 grams) all-purpose flour

¼ cups + 2 Tbs (75 grams) sugar

2 tsp (12 grams) salt

½ cup (120 ml) extra virgin olive oil

⅔ cup (150 grams) butter, at room temperature, for greasing the pan and shaping the dough

–

For the filling

2 cups (400 grams) sugar

4 Tbs ground cinnamon

½ tsp salt

–

For the glaze

¾ cup (100 grams) powdered sugar

2 tablespoons genuine maple syrup

1. Place the water, yeast, eggs, egg yolks, flour, sugar, and salt in the bowl of a stand mixer fitted with the dough hook and mix on a low speed for about 1 minute, until dough forms.

2. Increase the speed to medium low and knead for 5-7 minutes to a smooth, soft dough. Add the olive oil and knead until it's fully incorporated into the dough. Do not be afraid to over-knead.

3. Shape the dough into a ball and place in a greased bowl. Cover with a towel or a loose plastic wrap and let rise for 30 minutes at room temperature. Don't worry if the dough hasn't risen much.

4. Punch down the dough, cover, and let rise for another 30 minutes.

5. Grease the kubaneh pan or cake pan thoroughly and generously with butter.

6. Divide the dough into 8 equal pieces, roll into balls, and place on a greased plate. Brush the dough balls with butter and cover loosely with a plastic wrap. Let rest for 10 minutes.

7. **Prepare the filling:** Place the sugar, cinnamon, and salt in a mixing bowl.

8. Grease your hands and the worksurface with a spoonful of butter. Using your hands, press, flatten, and stretch a dough ball to a large rectangle, as thin as you possibly can, without tearing it.

→

9. Sprinkle ½–1 tablespoon of the sugar cinnamon mix evenly on the dough. Fold the sides toward the center, and then roll from the bottom to the top into a cylinder shape. Repeat this with the remaining dough balls.

10. Using a sharp knife, cut each cylinder in half, into 2 smaller cylinders, and place in an even layer in the kubaneh pan, cut side facing up. Continue until the pan is full and you've used all the dough.

11. Brush some butter on top of the unbaked kubaneh, cover, and let rise at room temperature for about 1 hour.

12. Preheat the oven to 100 °C (220 °F).

13. Cover the kubaneh with aluminum foil, making sure to leave the top loose to allow the dough to rise while baking.

14. Bake 8–10 hours. Every 2 hours or so, brush the kubaneh with 1–2 tablespoons of butter.

15. Release the kubaneh from the pan and place on a cooling rack.

16. **Prepare the glaze:** Mix the powdered sugar and maple syrup into a smooth cream. Spread the icing over the kubaneh.

Salads

Salads are an integral part of most Israeli meals, possibly because we have fresh, delicious vegetables that are available year-round. When I host brunches, I like to serve light salads that complement my baking, so here are two of my favorites.

EGG SALAD

Serves 4

-

- 6 hard-boiled eggs
- 1 onion, sliced and fried until deeply caramelized
- 1 Tbs mayonnaise
- ½ tsp mustard
- Sea salt, to taste
- Ground black pepper, to taste

1. Peel the eggs, chop, and place in a bowl.
2. Add the fried onion, mayonnaise, and mustard.
3. Season with salt and pepper and mix well. Taste and adjust the seasoning if necessary.

QUINOA SALAD

Serves 4

-

- ½ cup cooked quinoa
- 1 kohlrabi, peeled
- 1 beetroot, cooked and peeled
- ⅓ cup chopped parsley
- A handful of dried cranberries
- 1 Tbs lemon juice
- 1 Tbs extra virgin olive oil
- ½ tsp sea salt

1. Place all of the ingredients in a bowl and mix well. Taste and adjust the seasoning if necessary.
2. Feel free to play around and add seasonal produce such as filleted orange segments or snow peas.

BREAD PUDDING WITH *CRÈME ANGLAISE*: THE KING OF LEFTOVERS

The great thing about bread pudding is that you can make it from pretty much any pastry or baked good, and I mean anything: leftover bread or challah, baguettes, morning croissants and muffins, leftover babka; I've even created bread pudding from leftover pound cake. As I've mentioned before, I like making the most of leftovers.

So when is the right time to eat bread pudding? Bread pudding is great for weekend mornings, as a dessert for brunch, or even just as a nice snack to share with your friends if you're hosting a buffet. Whenever you want to serve it, bread pudding is a great way to reuse bread or pastries without throwing them out, and very easy to prepare and then to freeze for future use.

Makes 6 personal servings in 6 mini cocottes or muffin tins

-

For the bread base

3 cups stale 3-day-old bread, cut into 3-cm (1.2-in) cubes

1 cup chocolate chips and/or dried fruit, chopped

-

For the crème anglaise

1 1/4 cups (300 ml) milk

1 1/4 cups (300 ml) heavy cream

1/2 tsp pumpkin spice *(optional; see recipe on page 106)*

A pinch of salt

1/2 cup (100 grams) sugar

4 egg yolks

1/2 cup (113 grams) cold butter, cut into small cubes

1. **The night before:** Spread the bread cubes evenly in a deep baking dish. Sprinkle the chocolate chips and/or dried fruit.

2. **Prepare *crème anglaise*:** Place the milk, cream, salt, pumpkin spice (if using), and 1/4 cup (50 grams) of the sugar in a small pot and bring to a gentle simmer.

3. Beat the egg yolks and the remaining sugar in a separate bowl.

4. Add 2 tablespoons of the simmering milk mixture to the yolks and mix well.

5. Reduce to a low heat, add the yolk mixture to the milk mixture, and mix continuously until the custard thickens and leaves a path on the back of the mixing spoon when you draw a finger across it.

6. Divide the bread cubes between 6 mini cocottes or muffin tins.

7. Pour the custard over the bread cubes to cover. Cool to room temperature before covering with a plastic wrap and refrigerating overnight.

8. **The next day:** Preheat the oven to 180 °C (350 °F).

9. Sprinkle a few knobs of butter on each bread pudding and bake for 30 minutes, until the top is golden brown and crispy. Serve warm.

CLASSIC SCONES WITH CRANBERRIES

Scones are a quick bread that originated in Britain, possibly Scotland, which are made with leavened barley flour or white flour and buttermilk. Traditional scones are rolled into a round shape and cut into quarters before being baked on a griddle, although the recipes in this book use an oven instead. Scones are customarily eaten as part of afternoon tea and are usually served with jam and butter or clotted cream.

I don't remember the first time I ate a scone, but I know it was early in my childhood and it's remained one of my favorite pastries to this day. From a young age, my mom used to take me traveling a lot around the world, and one of the places we visited many times was London, which my mom loved (I remember she even considered living there for a time). My mom "infected" me with her love of everything British, starting with my never-ending appreciation of the British monarchy (I kid you not), English theatre, British music (have you ever noticed that some of the greatest musical creators of all time were British?), and their pastries.

Of course, when I was a child, London was not the culinary powerhouse that it is today, and my memories of the restaurants we went to on our visits were, to put it mildly, not good (in fact many of the meals were quite terrible). However, I also have beautiful memories of delicious, lavish breakfasts and of late-afternoon tea with my mom and my grandparents, where we experienced the full pomp and ceremony behind a full English tea. Tiny crustless sandwiches filled with butter and cucumber; little pastries; and, of course, scones.

Scones! Best eaten with whipped butter or with clotted cream together with the best jams I've ever tasted. The jams were usually made from one berry or another, and they were all delicious, so one didn't need to be choosy. Know this: if they're made correctly—and in the next two recipes I'm going to teach you how to make them correctly—the combination of scones and jam creates the "perfect bite."

Makes 8–10 scones

–

For the dough

2 1/3 cups (325 grams) bread flour

2 1/2 Tbs (20 grams) baking powder

1/4 cup (50 grams) sugar

A pinch of salt

1/2 cup (110 grams) cold butter, cut into cubes

1 cup (100 grams) dried cranberries

1 egg

1 egg yolk

About 1/2 cup (120 ml) heavy cream

–

For the topping

1/4 cup (60 ml) heavy cream

2 Tbs brown sugar

1. **The night before:** Place the flour, baking powder, sugar, salt, butter, and cranberries in the bowl of a stand mixer fitted with the paddle attachment and mix to a crumbly dough. Add the egg, yolk, and heavy cream, and mix until just combined (don't overmix).

2. Transfer the dough to a lightly floured worksurface and divide it into 2 equal pieces. Roll each piece into a ball, place on a parchment paper and flatten to a disc that is 1 cm (0.4 in) thick.

3. Using a dough scraper or a sharp knife, cut each disc into 8–10 wedges. Place the scones in an airtight container, using parchment paper to separate between them to prevent them from sticking. Freeze overnight.

4. The next morning, preheat the oven to 180 °C (350 °F).

5. Arrange the scones approximately 6 centimeters (2–3 inches) apart on a baking tray lined with parchment paper.

6. Brush the scones with the heavy cream and sprinkle brown sugar on top.

7. Bake 15-25 minutes, until the scones are lightly golden.

8. Serve warm with whipped cream and jam.

A Baker's Tip

Why should you freeze scones?

There are a lot of cookies that respond better to the baking process if they're first cooled or frozen. This is because they contain a large amount of butter, and chilling the dough (which hardens the butter) prevents the butter from "escaping" after the dough is placed in the oven. As a result, the pastry keeps its shape better. With scones, one of my favorite things is that you can prepare relatively large quantities and keep the unbaked scones in a box in the freezer. When you want to serve them, just place them on a baking tray and bake them. This makes them incredibly convenient to serve, so you're always ready with a tasty, fresh pastry, ready to be eaten!

Fruit Jams
(page 66)

SAVORY PARMESAN SCONES

A few years ago, I was working as a pastry chef at Pronto, one of the best-known restaurants in Tel Aviv. Among other things, Pronto hosts private events, and for one of these events, I was asked to make scones. Instead of making traditional scones, I decided to make savory scones with Parmesan cheese. When my chef, David Frenkel, tasted the scones, he loved them, and asked me to prepare them as an integral part of our bread basket. However, after realizing that preparing the scones—while not complicated—was rather time-consuming, David decided to include them only in the weekend bread basket.

From then on, every weekend we baked and served savory, fluffy Parmesan scones as part of the weekend bread basket. About one-third of the scones I baked found their way into the stomachs of the wait staff, while the rest, on good days, would finally be delivered to our customers, who were immediately hooked.

Makes 16 scones

-

For the dough

2 cups + 2 Tbs (300 grams) all-purpose flour

1 Tbs (8 grams) baking powder

1/4 tsp baking soda

2 1/2 Tbs (30 grams) sugar

1 tsp salt

1/2 cup + 1 Tbs (130 grams) cold butter, cut into cubes

1/3 cup (70 ml) heavy cream

3 oz (90 grams) *crème fraîche*

2 1/2 cups (225 grams) Parmesan cheese, grated

1/2 tsp ground black pepper

-

For the topping

5 Tbs heavy cream

3 Tbs Parmesan cheese, grated

1. **The night before:** Place the flour, baking powder, sugar, salt, and diced butter in the bowl of a stand mixer fitted with the paddle attachment and mix to a crumbly dough. Add the heavy cream and crème fraîche, and mix until just combined (avoid overmixing). Add the grated Parmesan and black pepper.

2. Roll the dough into a ball, place between 2 sheets of parchment paper and flatten to a 2–3-cm (1-in)-thick disc. Place in the refrigerator overnight.

3. **The next day:** Using a dough scraper or a sharp knife, cut the disc into 8 wedges. Place the scones in an airtight container, using parchment paper to separate between them to prevent them from sticking, and freeze until ready to bake.

4. Preheat the oven to 180 °C (350 °F) and line a baking tray with parchment paper.

5. Arrange the scones approximately 6 centimeters (2–3 inches) apart, brush with heavy cream, and sprinkle grated Parmesan on top.

6. Bake for 10 minutes, until the scones are lightly golden. Cool on a rack.

BASIC FRUIT JAM

Let me tell you a little secret: Ever since I was a little kid, I haven't been a fan of jams or jellies. On Hanukkah (the Festival of Lights), I would eat *suffganiot* (jelly donuts) with *dulce de leche* (which is like caramel) rather than the traditional strawberry jelly. Having said that, I'm even more of a fan of avoiding waste, so I began making jams when I realized that fruit was about to go bad and I really didn't want to just toss it away. I began to make jam to use it in my baking or with scones, like the jams they used to serve with the scones we ate in England. These jams aren't hard to make and are worth having in your kitchen for all occasions.

The quantities below make a 16-fl-oz (473-ml) jar, but don't limit yourself: If you have more fruit (or less), just remember that the sugar is half the amount in weight of the fruit, so if you have half the amount of fruit, just use half the amount of sugar, and feel free to multiply the quantities if you have more fruit.

Makes a 16-fl-oz (473-ml) jar

-

1 lb (500 grams) fruit of your choice

1 1/4 cups (250 grams) sugar

1/2 lemon, juiced

1. Place the fruit, sugar, and lemon juice in a pot and leave uncovered at room temperature for 30 minutes.

2. Cook over a low heat, occasionally stirring, and bring to a gentle simmer. Cook 1–2 hours, until the liquids have reduced to a thick jam.

3. Once cooled, keep refrigerated.

Jam Variations

Feel free to add a sliced vanilla pod, cinnamon stick, star anise, or a pinch of salt. If you want to add tartness, try adding freshly-squeezed lemon or lime juice or a few drops of yuzu.

Ø 70 mm

Egg Salad (page 57)

Scrambled Eggs Done Right

SCRAMBLED EGGS DONE RIGHT

Believe it or not, setting aside all of the wonderful baking possibilities, I think that the perfect breakfast is scrambled eggs on toast. When I was quite young, my mom taught me how to make scrambled eggs, and then I perfected them on my own, so that I was the one who would make scrambled eggs for everyone else. It drives me crazy when people overcook the eggs, which is why I decided to include my scrambled eggs recipe in this baking book. Now you'll have no more excuses for making scrambled eggs that are anything less than DELICIOUS.

First, remember that scrambled eggs need patience, like anything in life worth waiting for. Scrambled eggs should be the last thing you make before sitting down to eat; the entire meal should be ready and the table set, and the eggs should be enjoyed while they're still hot.

Serves 1 (double the quantities if you want to share)

-

2 eggs

A pinch of salt

1 Tbs (15 grams) Parmesan cheese, grated

2 Tbs (30 grams) butter

1. Melt the butter in a non-stick frying pan over medium heat.

2. Place the eggs, salt, and grated Parmesan in a bowl and beat briskly with a whisk.

3. When the butter has melted, pour the eggs into the frying pan, and immediately scramble with a wooden spoon.

4. I like my scrambled eggs still runny and moist, so I turn off the heat when they're about 90 percent cooked.

5. Serve immediately.

Butternut Squash
Bread Roll
(page 82)

Egg Salad
(page 57)
Potato Bread Roll
(page 85)
Quinoa Salad
(page 57)
Scrambled Eggs
Done Right
(page 71)

Section 3

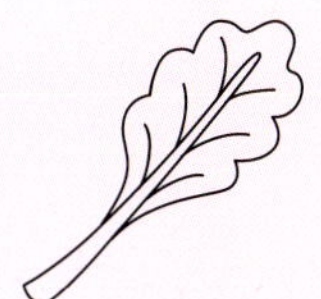

Seasonal Recipes

Sometimes seasons seem to last forever (like an Israeli summer), but sometimes they're short and sweet, and you just have to take advantage of the seasonal products that become available for such a short time, such as strawberries, asparagus, green garlic, apricots (in spring), or mushrooms (in fall).

Of course, nowadays you can probably get seasonal produce year-round; for me, however, the following recipes will always evoke a specific time of year. Having spent time in New York, I think of autumn as being all about pumpkins and apple-picking, since apple pies are best with freshly-picked apples. And rhubarb is best in spring to early summer.

Rhubarb is a seasonal plant that most Israelis have never heard of and have never eaten. Rhubarb looks a lot like celery, but when it's ripe it's a bright pink-red. In Israel you'll find it somewhere between red and green. Rhubarb stalks are safe to eat, even raw, but they're very tart. The leaves, however, contain a chemical called oxalic acid that, when consumed in large quantities, can be fatal.

While working at Pronto (a famous Italian restaurant in Tel Aviv), I persuaded the farmers to bring me as much rhubarb as they could lay their hands on, and I would make a rhubarb marmalade for a strawberry-rhubarb dessert that we served that winter in the restaurant.

RHUBARB TART WITH MARZIPAN

Strawberries and rhubarb are a really great combination, but since strawberry season in Israel is in winter and doesn't coincide with rhubarb season, I decided to make a rhubarb and marzipan cream tart. If you have any rhubarb left over after making the tart, don't throw it away—just turn it into jam (*see recipe on page 66*).

Makes one 20–24-cm (8–10-in) tart pan

–

For the crust

1 1/4 cups (156 grams) all-purpose flour

1/2 Tbs sugar

1/2 tsp salt

1/2 cup (110 grams) cold butter, cut into small cubes

1/4 Tbs vinegar mixed in 1 cup of cold water

–

For the marzipan cream

6 Tbs (85 grams) butter, at room temperature

6 oz (170 grams) marzipan/almond paste (available online and in specialty shops), chopped

1 egg

1 Tbs (10 grams) cornstarch

2 tsp (10 ml) rum

1 bunch rhubarb stalks, washed and trimmed

Powdered sugar, for dusting

1. **Prepare the crust:** Place the flour, sugar, salt, and butter in the bowl of a stand mixer fitted with the paddle attachment, and mix to a texture resembling coarse meal. Pour the vinegar-water slowly and while mixing continuously, just until the dough comes together. You may not need to use all of the water.

2. Roll into a ball, flatten to a disc, and cover in plastic wrap. Refrigerate for at least 1 hour.

3. Place the dough between two sheets of parchment paper and roll into a circle. Transfer to the tart pan and press to the bottom and sides of the pan. Place in the freezer until ready to use.

4. **Prepare the marzipan cream:** Place the butter and marzipan in the bowl of a stand mixer fitted with the paddle attachment, and mix until the marzipan has fully incorporated the butter. This may take several minutes. Add the egg and beat to a smooth cream. Add the cornstarch and rum and mix well.

5. On parchment paper, draw a circle the diameter of the tart pan, and divide the circle into quarters. Trim the rhubarb stalks to shorter pieces, using longer pieces to frame each quarter and shorter pieces to fill them in. Set aside.

6. Preheat the oven to 170 °C (340 °F).

7. Pour the filling into the frozen tart crust and spread evenly. Then, arrange the rhubarb pieces on top of the cream based on the template you created.

9. Dust powdered sugar on top and bake for 30–40 minutes, until the crust and the marzipan cream are golden. Cool to room temperature.

Ombré Apple Pie
(page 80)

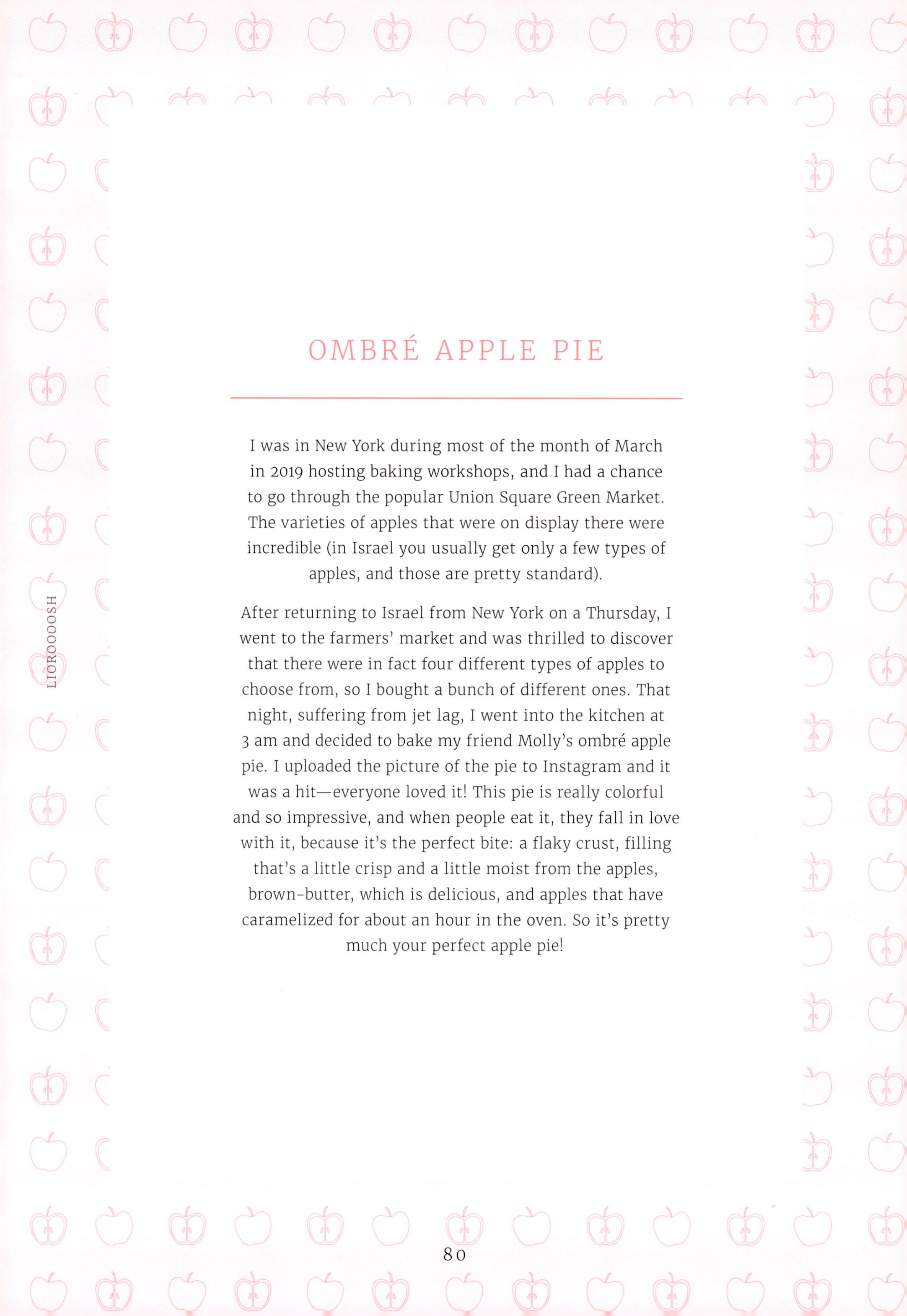

OMBRÉ APPLE PIE

I was in New York during most of the month of March in 2019 hosting baking workshops, and I had a chance to go through the popular Union Square Green Market. The varieties of apples that were on display there were incredible (in Israel you usually get only a few types of apples, and those are pretty standard).

After returning to Israel from New York on a Thursday, I went to the farmers' market and was thrilled to discover that there were in fact four different types of apples to choose from, so I bought a bunch of different ones. That night, suffering from jet lag, I went into the kitchen at 3 am and decided to bake my friend Molly's ombré apple pie. I uploaded the picture of the pie to Instagram and it was a hit—everyone loved it! This pie is really colorful and so impressive, and when people eat it, they fall in love with it, because it's the perfect bite: a flaky crust, filling that's a little crisp and a little moist from the apples, brown-butter, which is delicious, and apples that have caramelized for about an hour in the oven. So it's pretty much your perfect apple pie!

Makes one 24–26-cm (9–10-in) pie dish

-

For the crust

2 1/2 cups (350 grams) all-purpose flour

1 Tbs sugar

1 tsp fine salt

1 cup (220 grams) cold butter, cut into cubes

1/4 Tbs vinegar mixed in 1 cup of cold water

1 beaten egg, for brushing

Brown sugar, for sprinkling

-

For the filling

1/2 quantity almond cream (*see recipe on pages 223–224*)

1 red apple such as Red Delicious, washed, cored, and thinly sliced

1 Pink Lady apple, washed, cored, and thinly sliced

1 Golden Delicious apple, washed, cored, and thinly sliced

1 green apple, such as Granny Smith, washed, cored, and thinly sliced

-

For the brown-butter caramel

1/2 cup (100 grams) butter

1/2 cup (100 grams) sugar

1/2 tsp salt

2 Tbs heavy cream

1. **Prepare the pie crust:** Place the flour, salt, sugar, and butter in the bowl of a stand mixer fitted with the paddle attachment, and mix to a texture resembling coarse meal.

2. Pour the vinegar-water slowly and while mixing continuously, just until the dough comes together. You may not need to use all of the water.

3. Roll into a ball, flatten to a disc, and cover in plastic wrap. Refrigerate for at least 1 hour.

4. Place the dough between two sheets of parchment paper and roll out into a circle that's 5 mm (about 0.2 in) thick, 26–28 cm (10–11 in) in diameter. Transfer to the tart pan and press to the bottom and sides of the pan. Place in the freezer until ready to use.

5. Spread a thin, even layer of the almond cream on the frozen pie crust. Refrigerate.

6. Arrange the apple slices tightly in concentric circles. Refrigerate.

7. **Prepare the brown-butter:** Melt the butter in a small pot over medium heat. As the butter melts it will begin to foam and gradually turn a toasty brown color and release a nutty aroma. Take off the heat and transfer to a bowl to cool.

8. **Prepare the caramel:** Place the sugar in a pan over medium heat and cook until the sugar dissolves to a clear syrup. Continue to cook the syrup until it turns to an amber color. Add the salt and the heavy cream and mix well. Take off the heat.

9. Drizzle the caramel and brown-butter over the apples.

10. Brush the pie crust with the beaten egg and sprinkle the brown sugar. Transfer to the refrigerator and preheat the oven to 180 °C (350 °F).

12. Bake for 50-60 minutes until the pie crust is golden and the caramel is bubbling. Cool to room temperature.

13. Serve warm or at room temperature alongside ice cream or crème fraîche.

BUTTERNUT SQUASH BREAD ROLLS

Makes 8 rolls

–

For the starter

5 ½ Tbs (55 grams) bread flour

3 Tbs (45 ml) water

A pinch of instant dry yeast

–

For the dough

1 kg (2.2 lb) whole butternut squash (or pumpkin) or 850 grams (1.9 lb) diced squash

6 ½ cups (790 grams) bread flour

1 ¼ tsp (25 grams) salt

2 tsp (8 grams) active dry yeast

3.5 oz (100 grams) starter (see recipe above)

3 Tbs (45 ml) extra virgin olive oil

3–4 garlic cloves (30 grams), chopped, lightly fried, and cooled

⅔ cup (15 grams) parsley, chopped

–

For brushing

1 beaten egg

1. **To make the starter (at least one day before):** Place the flour, water, and yeast in a bowl and mix with a fork. Place in an airtight container at room temperature and let rest 14–16 hours prior to making the dough.

2. **To prepare the butternut squash:** Preheat the oven to 180 °C (350 °F) and line a baking tray with parchment paper. If using whole squash, peel it and remove the seeds and insides. Cut into large chunks, even in size.

3. Drizzle the diced squash with olive oil, season with a little salt, and roast until soft. Cool to room temperature.

4. **To prepare the dough:** Place the flour, roasted butternut squash, salt, yeast, and starter in the bowl of a stand mixer fitted with the dough hook. Mix on a low speed until the dough comes together. Increase the speed and knead for 10 minutes, until you have a soft, smooth dough.

5. Reduce to a low speed, add the olive oil, and knead until it's fully incorporated into the dough. Add the fried garlic and parsley, and mix well.

6. Shape the dough into a ball and place in a greased bowl. Cover with a towel or a loose plastic wrap and let rise for 45 minutes at room temperature.

7. Punch down the dough, cover, and let rise for another 45 minutes.

8. Divide the dough into 7-oz (200-gram) pieces and roll into balls. Cover and let rise for 10 minutes. Reshape the rolls and place on a baking tray lined with parchment paper. Cover and let rise for 30–40 minutes at room temperature.

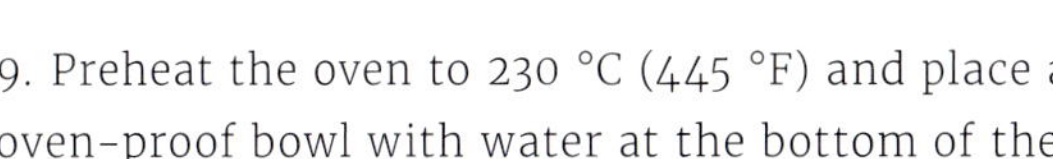

9. Preheat the oven to 230 °C (445 °F) and place an oven-proof bowl with water at the bottom of the oven to create a humid environment.

10. Brush the rolls with the beaten egg. Then, using a lightly floured sharp knife or scissors, score an 'X' on top of each roll.

11. Bake for 15 minutes, until golden brown.

POTATO BREAD ROLLS VARIATION

1. In step 4 of the Butternut Squash Bread Rolls recipe (*see page 82*), omit the butternut squash and add **1 1/2 cups (350 ml) of water** to the dough.

2. In step 5, add **1 3/4 cups (585 grams) of potato** that has been diced, roasted, and cooled, along with the fried **garlic** and **parsley**. You can substitute the parsley with chopped **rosemary** or **thyme** (optional).

Pumpkin Spice Scones with Chocolate Chunk and Maple Glaze *(page 88)*

I want to share with you a recipe for one of my favorite pastries in the world, the scone, which, in the spirit of seasonal baking, I've combined with pumpkin. Scones don't get the appreciation they deserve in Israel, and indeed there are only a few places here that make scones (actually most of them have their own interpretation of scones but they're really very different from the original). So many people here continue to wonder: What's so special about this pastry?

But, if you're like me, and have spent a significant part of your life in countries that serve scones (like England, the United States, and Canada), you can appreciate this pastry and understand what makes it special. In England, scones are served plain with clotted cream and berry jam on the side, and they are mouth-wateringly good. At the Levain Bakery on the Upper East Side, people stand in line to get their scones—stuffed with chocolate chips or peanut butter icicles or even raisins. In Japan you'll find variations of scones with matcha tea, and if you're lucky, scones with *azuki* sweet red bean paste.

I love scones in every possible way, with any combination, but to be honest, I prefer them with butter alone. Scones are **not** a complicated pastry and are fairly easy to make. The dough needs to be flaky and not too dry, and a perfect balance of sweet and salty because scones are not a sweet pastry. This recipe, unlike my classic scone recipe (*see page 60*), is for pumpkin-chocolate-chunk scones, with a gorgeous maple syrup glaze. Now, I'm pretty sure you're going to get immediately addicted—so don't say I didn't warn you!

PUMPKIN SPICE SCONES WITH CHOCOLATE CHUNK AND MAPLE GLAZE

Makes 8 scones

-

For the dough

2 1/3 cups (325 grams) all-purpose flour

5 tsp (20 grams) baking powder

4 Tbs (45 grams) sugar

A pinch of salt

1 tsp pumpkin spice (*see recipe on page 106*)

1/2 cup (110 grams) cold butter, cut into cubes

2/3 cup (100 grams) dark chocolate chips

1 egg

1 egg yolk

2/3 cup (140 grams) pumpkin puree (*see recipe on page 107*)

-

For the topping

1/2 cup (120 ml) heavy cream

1 Tbs brown sugar

1/2 tsp sea salt (optional)

-

For the maple glaze

1/2 cup (60 grams) powdered sugar

3 Tbs maple syrup

1. **The night before:** Place the flour, baking powder, sugar, salt, pumpkin spice, diced butter, and chocolate chips in the bowl of a stand mixer fitted with the paddle attachment, and mix to a crumbly dough. Add the egg, yolk, and pumpkin puree, and mix until just combined (avoid overmixing).

2. Roll the dough into a ball, place between 2 sheets of parchment paper, and flatten to a 2–3-cm (1-in)-thick disc.

3. Using a dough scraper or a sharp knife, cut the disc into 8 wedges. Place the scones in an airtight container, using parchment paper to separate between them to prevent them from sticking. Freeze overnight (*to learn why you freeze scones, see page 61*).

4. **The next morning:** Preheat the oven to 180 °C (350 °F).

5. Arrange the scones approximately 6 centimeters (2–3 inches) apart on a baking tray lined with parchment paper.

6. Brush the scones with the heavy cream and then sprinkle the sugar and (optional) salt on top.

7. Bake for 15 minutes, until the scones are lightly golden. Cool on a rack.

8. **Prepare the maple glaze:** Place the powdered sugar and maple syrup in a bowl and mix well. Use a spoon to drizzle the glaze over the cooled scones.

9. The scones taste best the same day they are baked but will keep at room temperature for up to 3 days in an airtight container.

Section 4

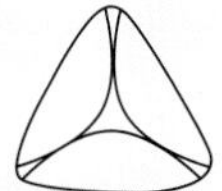

Holiday-Inspired Baking

In this section I've pulled together recipes that are great for specific holidays, although honestly, you don't need a holiday as an excuse to make any of these.

One Rosh Hashanah, while I was studying in New York, I drove to the country, to attend a holiday dinner at my brother's friend's cabin in upstate New York. Each person had a role: I was supposed to bring *gefilte* fish (a traditional Jewish dish that's made from a poached mixture of ground deboned fish) from Citarella, a gourmet food market on the Upper West Side that also sells ready-made food. We had a ride from the city, so we drove first to Citarella, and then to the cabin.

As we were preparing the meal, we realized that we didn't have a dessert or anything with apples and honey (apples are traditionally dipped in honey on Rosh Hashanah to symbolize a sweet new year). So I said I'd take care of it: I took some apples and began to caramelize them in honey, and I essentially made this apple cobbler and then added crumble on top. Everyone there was really impressed that without any planning or additional shopping, I'd managed to pull off an entire dessert within an hour, and just in time for our Rosh Hashanah dinner!

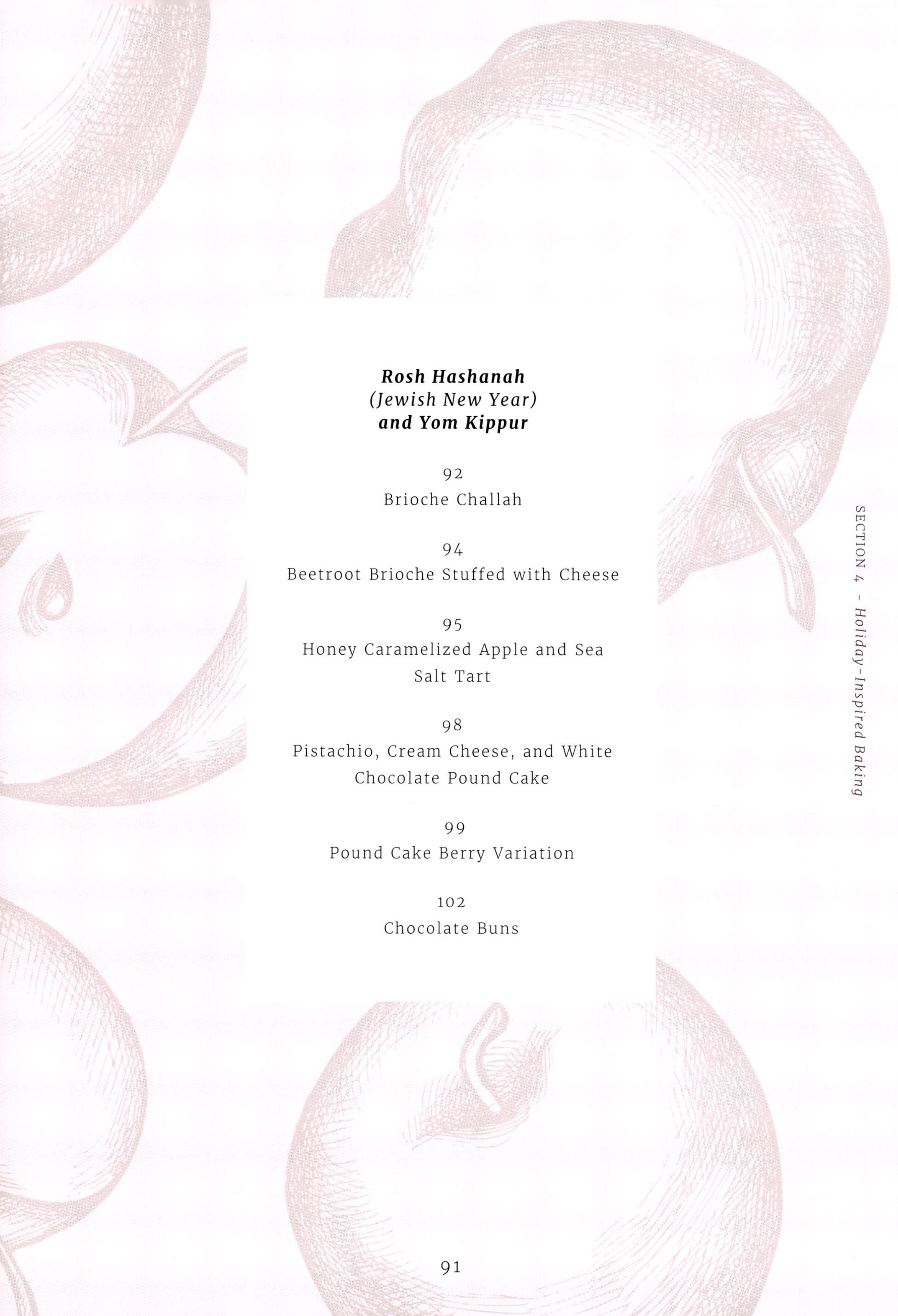

Rosh Hashanah
(Jewish New Year)
and Yom Kippur

BRIOCHE CHALLAH

My challahs are always rich and flaky, but this one is truly a celebration, using a brioche dough that melts in your mouth. You don't need a holiday as an excuse for making it, but it's definitely perfect for Rosh Hashanah.

Makes 2 brioche challahs

–

For the dough

3 ½ cups (500 grams) bread flour

2 tsp (8 grams) active dry yeast

½ cup (110 ml) water, at room temperature

3 ½ Tbs (50 ml) cold milk

2 eggs

¼ cup + 1 Tbs (60 grams) sugar

1 Tbs (10 grams) salt

⅔ cups (160 grams) cold butter cut into cubes

–

For the topping

1 beaten egg, for brushing

Pearl sugar

1. **The night before:** Place the flour, yeast, water, milk, and eggs in the bowl of a stand mixer fitted with the dough hook and mix on a low speed for 2 minutes. Add the sugar and the salt, increase the speed slightly, and knead for 10 minutes, until you have a soft, smooth dough.

2. Add the butter cubes and knead until they're fully incorporated into the dough. The dough should be smooth and shiny. Occasionally scrape the sides of the bowl.

3. Shape the dough into a ball and transfer to a greased bowl. Cover with a towel or a loose plastic wrap and let rise in the refrigerator overnight.

4. **The next day:** Place the dough on a lightly floured surface and divide into 10 equal pieces, each weighing about 3.5 oz (100 grams). Roll into balls, cover with a towel, and let rest for 5 minutes.

5. Grease and line a loaf pan with parchment paper.

6. Roll the balls and place in the loaf pan in an even layer.

7. Brush a thin coat of the beaten egg and let rise uncovered at room temperature for 1 hour.

8. Brush the loaf with the beaten egg, sprinkle pearl sugar on top, and then preheat the oven to 180 °C (350 °F), allowing the challah to rise in the meantime.

9. Bake for 20–25 minutes, until the challah is a deep, even shade of golden brown. Cool on a rack.

BEETROOT BRIOCHE STUFFED WITH CHEESE

Makes 1 brioche loaf

–

For the dough

3 ½ cups (500 grams) bread flour

2 tsp (7 grams) active dry yeast

½ cup (110 grams) roasted beetroot puree (*see recipe on page 26*)

2 ½ Tbs (40 ml) milk, lukewarm

2 eggs

¼ cup + 1 Tbs (60 grams) sugar

1 Tbs (10 grams) salt

⅔ cup (160 grams) cold butter, cut into cubes

–

For the cheese filling

10.5 oz (300 grams) Gorgonzola/blue cheese

28.8 oz (50 grams) feta cheese

–

For the topping

1 beaten egg, for brushing

Pearl sugar, black sesame, or poppy seeds

1. **The night before:** Place the flour, yeast, beetroot puree, milk, and eggs in the bowl of a stand mixer fitted with the dough hook and mix on the lowest speed for 2 minutes. Add the sugar and the salt, increase the speed by 1, and knead for 10 minutes, until you have a soft, smooth dough.

2. Add the butter cubes and knead until they're fully incorporated into the dough. The dough should be smooth and shiny. Occasionally scrape the sides of the bowl.

3. Shape the dough into a ball and transfer to a greased bowl. Cover with a towel or a loose plastic wrap and let rise in the refrigerator overnight.

4. **Prepare the cheese filling:** Place the cheese in a bowl or a blender and mix to a smooth paste. Transfer to a piping bag and keep refrigerated until ready to use.

5. **The next day:** Place the dough on a lightly floured surface and divide into equal pieces, each weighing 3.5 oz (100 grams). Roll each piece out into a circle 5 mm (0.2 in) thick and pipe a teaspoon of the cheese filling in the center. Gently fold the dough over the filling and roll into a ball. Repeat with the remaining dough and filling.

6. Grease and line a loaf pan with parchment paper. Place the dough balls in the pan with the seam facing down, cover, and let rise at room temperature for 1 hour.

7. Preheat the oven to 180 °C (350 °F).

8. Brush the loaf with the beaten egg, and sprinkle pearl sugar, black sesame, or poppy seeds.

9. Bake for 45–50 minutes, until the brioche is a deep, even shade of golden brown. Cool on a rack.

HONEY CARAMELIZED APPLE AND SEA SALT TART

While my last-minute apple cobbler/crumble (*see page 90*) was something I put together with little notice, this tart is a beautiful, perfect dessert you'll want to serve any day, and especially on holidays.

Makes one 24-cm (9.5-in) tart pan

-

For the crust

1 cup + 4 Tbs (180 grams) all-purpose flour

1 ¼ Tbs (15 grams) sugar

½ tsp salt

½ cup (110 grams) cold butter, cut into small cubes

¼ Tbs vinegar mixed in 1 cup of cold water

-

For the filling

3 apples, Golden or Red Delicious, peeled, cored, and cut into 8 wedges each

2 Tbs honey

1 Tbs (15 grams) butter

-

For the honey cream

2 Tbs (30 grams) melted butter

¾ cup (150 grams) sugar

1 Tbs cornstarch

½ tsp vanilla extract

¼ tsp salt

About ½ cup (150 grams) honey

1 egg

1 egg yolk

¼ cup (60 ml) heavy cream

1 Tbs vinegar

-

To serve

Sea salt flakes or powdered sugar

1. **Prepare the crust:** Place the flour, salt, sugar, and butter in the bowl of a stand mixer fitted with the paddle attachment, and mix to a texture resembling coarse meal.

2. Pour the vinegar-water slowly and while mixing continuously, just until the dough comes together. You may not need to use all of the water.

3. Roll into a ball, flatten to a disc, and cover in plastic wrap. Refrigerate for at least 1 hour.

4. Place the dough between two sheets of parchment paper and roll into a circle that's 5 mm (0.2 in) thick, 26 cm (10 in) in diameter. Transfer to the tart pan and press to the bottom and sides of the pan. Place in the freezer until ready to use.

→

5. **Prepare the filling:** Place the honey in a small pot and bring to a simmer. Add the butter and mix until fully melted. Add the apple wedges and cook over a low heat for 10 minutes, until golden and soft. Drain the apples and preserve the liquids for the glaze.

6. **Prepare the honey cream:** Place the melted butter, sugar, cornstarch, and vanilla extract in a bowl and mix well. Add the honey and mix. Add the eggs, heavy cream, and vinegar, and mix to a smooth, runny cream.

7. Preheat the oven to 180 °C (350 °F).

8. Arrange the apple wedges in the frozen tart crust in concentric circles, starting from the outside and working your way to the center. Pour the honey cream on top to cover.

9. Bake for 40 minutes, until the cream is set and golden.

10. Sprinkle sea salt or powdered sugar on top and cool to room temperature.

11. **Prepare the glaze:** Place the apple cooking juices in a small pot and cook until the volume is reduced by half. Cool to room temperature and serve alongside the tart.

PISTACHIO, CREAM CHEESE, AND WHITE CHOCOLATE POUND CAKE

I have a basic recipe for pound cake with cream cheese, and since I love its texture, I use that basic recipe and add different ingredients to make different pound cakes.

I also love to use pistachios, so I decided to add a swirl of pistachio paste to the cake—and it was a hit! The recipe initially was off the cuff—a kind of improvisation—but people kept asking me for the recipe, and I realized I had to write it down to save it. I also realized I wanted to share it with the world properly, so I kept it for this book. It's a super easy cake that you can store outside of the refrigerator, but of course, it usually gets eaten on the same day, so that particular issue rarely comes up. Anyway, it's one of my personal favorites, and my customers love it too.

Makes 2 cake loaves

–

For the batter

14 Tbs (200 grams) butter, at room temperature

1 1/2 cups (300 grams) sugar

1/2 tsp salt

4 eggs

1 brick cream cheese or about 1 cup (250 grams) mascarpone cheese

3 cups (420 grams) all-purpose flour

2 1/2 tsp (10 grams) baking powder

7 oz (200 grams) sour cream

3.5 oz (100 grams) pistachio paste (pistachio praline, available online and at specialty shops)

2/3 cup (100 grams) white chocolate chips

–

For the glaze

1 cup (130 grams) powdered sugar

4 Tbs maple syrup

1. Preheat the oven to 180 °C (350 °F). Grease and line 2 loaf pans with parchment paper.

2. Place the butter, salt, and sugar in the bowl of a stand mixer fitted with the paddle attachment, and beat until light and fluffy.

3. Add the eggs, one at a time, and beat after each addition until the egg is fully incorporated.

4. Add the cream cheese (or mascarpone), flour, baking powder, and sour cream, and mix until just combined (avoid overmixing).

5. Fold the chocolate chips into the batter. Add the pistachio paste and fold only once or twice, to create a marbled effect.

6. Divide the batter between the cake pans and smooth the top with a spatula.

7. Bake for 30–40 minutes, until a toothpick inserted in the center comes out clean. Let the cakes cool in the pans for about 10 minutes before releasing them and transferring to a wire rack.

8. **Once the cake has cooled to room temperature, prepare the glaze:** Mix the powdered sugar and maple into a smooth paste. Pour over the cakes and let the icing set for 10 minutes.

POUND CAKE BERRY VARIATION

For a berry cream cheese pound cake, substitute the pistachio paste and white chocolate chips with **1 cup of berries** of your choice.

Don't forget to toss the berries with **1 tablespoon of flour** so that they don't sink to the bottom of the loaf.

Pistachio, Cream Cheese, and White Chocolate Pound Cake (page 98)
Marble Cake (page 189)

Pound Cake
Berry Variation
(page 99)

CHOCOLATE BUNS

These chocolate buns are made with cocoa and chocolate chunk. Add a light spread of creamy butter, take a single bite and I promise: you'll feel like you're in heaven!

Makes 10 buns

–

For the dough

3 2/3 cups (520 grams) bread flour

3 1/2 Tbs (35 grams) cocoa powder

4 tsp (15 grams) active dry yeast

1/4 cup (50 grams) sugar

2 Tbs (40 grams) date molasses or date honey

1 cup (240 ml) water

1/2 cup + 1 Tbs (140 ml) milk

3 1/2 Tbs (50 grams) butter, softened

2/3 cup (100 grams) dark chocolate with a minimum of 60% cocoa solids, chopped

–

For the topping

1 beaten egg, for brushing

Pearl sugar

1. Place the bread flour, cocoa powder, yeast, sugar, date molasses, water, milk, and butter in the bowl of a stand mixer fitted with the paddle attachment, and mix on a low speed until the dough comes together. Increase the speed slightly and knead for 10 minutes, until you have a soft, smooth dough.

2. Add the chopped chocolate and mix until it's incorporated into the dough.

3. Transfer the dough to a greased bowl, cover, and let rise for 40 minutes.

4. Place the dough on a lightly floured worksurface and divide into 10 equal balls, each weighing about 3.8 oz (110 grams). Cover and let rest for 10 minutes.

5. Shape into smooth dough balls and place in a baking tray lined with parchment paper, leaving plenty of room between them. Brush with the beaten egg and let rise for 30–40 minutes.

6. Preheat the oven to 180 °C (350 °F).

7. Brush the buns with the beaten egg and sprinkle pearl sugar on top.

8. Bake for 10–15 minutes. Cool on a wire rack.

I celebrated my first Thanksgiving with my "adoptive" American family. I should explain what I mean by adoptive, since I actually had family (my brother Amit and his then-girlfriend now-wife, Sigal) who were also living in New York, but my adoptive family was this great Israeli couple who'd moved there many years ago, Joe (Yossi) and Michal.

I met Joe and Michal, of all places, through my gym. When I first moved to New York, I decided it was really important for me to maintain my daily routine, and that included working out on a regular basis. When I joined this gym, I explained that I was a student and that I was studying the art of pastry, so I really needed a gym that would be within my limited budget. I happened to find a gym manager who was French, who was really excited about the fact that I was studying to make fine pastries, so I started to bring little treats from my studies: macarons, cookies, and cakes that I knew the staff would enjoy. The recipients of my goodies wanted to find a way to thank me for them, so they offered a training session with a personal trainer. I told them they really didn't have to do anything in return, but they insisted, and that's how I met Joe—at my personal training session. At first, Joe looked like this big, scary guy, because he's a body builder (I guess he would appear pretty scary to anyone who didn't know him). Later, I discovered that, like many big guys, he's just a big Care Bear, and it didn't take long for him to make me feel truly welcome.

Joe became much more than my personal trainer; I think it was just inevitable that he and his family would "adopt" me, and very quickly his entire family became my family. They would invite me to Shabbat meals and to cholent (a traditional meat stew meal), and then, of course, they invited me to holidays, including Thanksgiving. Even today, when I visit New York, we make dinner plans, and we get together when they visit Israel as well.

On Thanksgiving Day, I went to their house, and Michal and I drove to the supermarket to get the final touches for the dinner (unlike in Israel, where supermarkets close early on a holiday evening, so there's no chance of getting anything last minute). I remember the turkey we had to cook was enormous, because there were so many people coming; it must have weighed 20 pounds! Michal took the turkey out of the brine and placed it in the oven, and that was the first time I saw the rack they use to make the turkey. We started cooking and baking first thing that morning, and I must have made a million pies, because that's what people do on Thanksgiving. It was so cool, and I really enjoyed it, and even today, I get a reminder from Facebook that shows a post with a picture of Michal and me looking at the turkey from above—as though we're trying to figure out how to fit it into the oven!

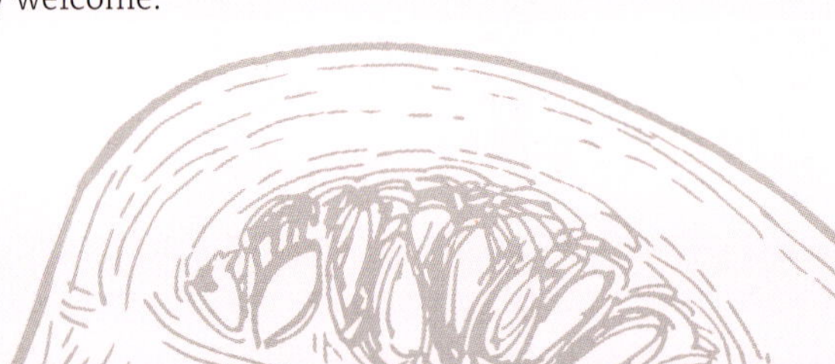

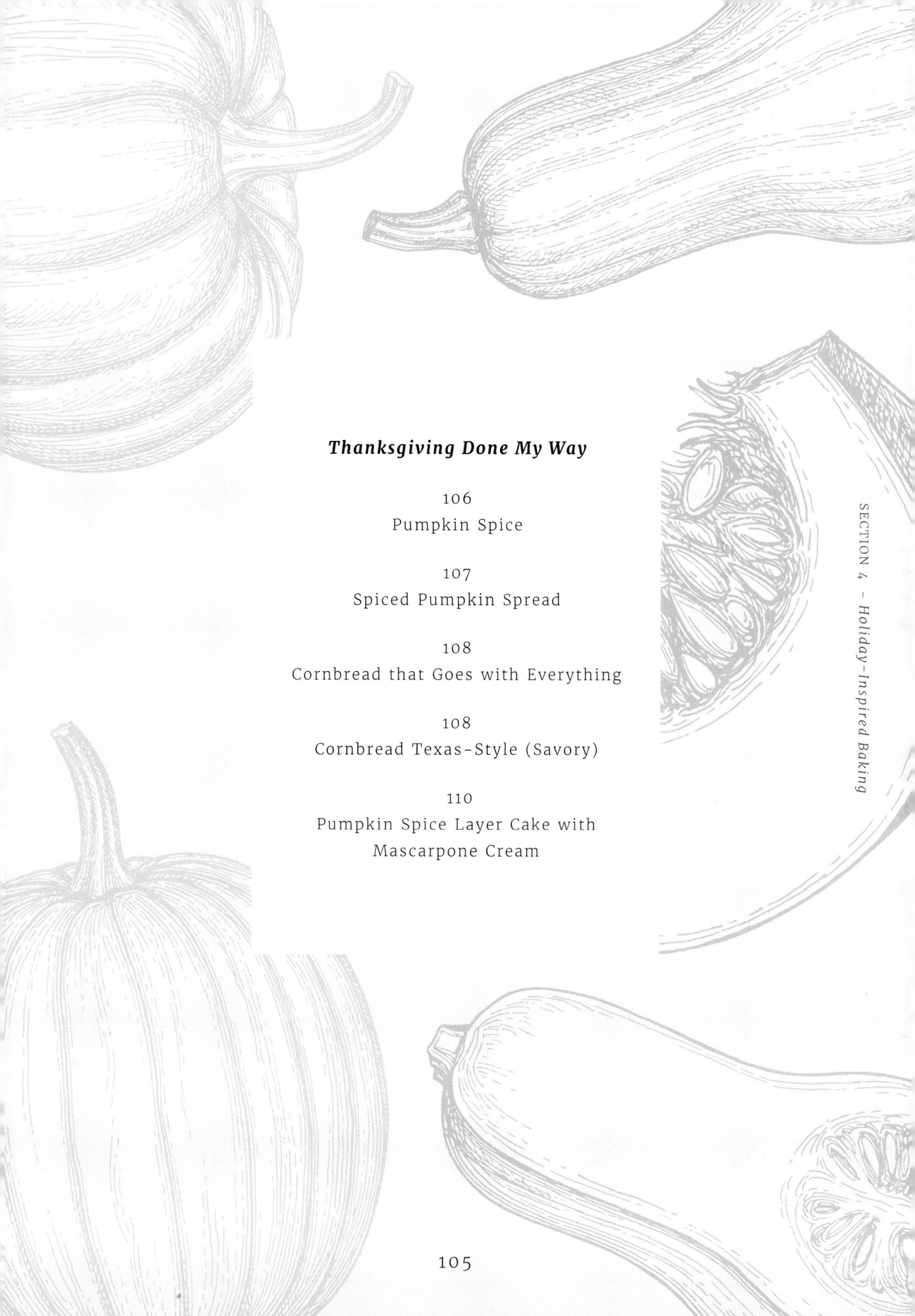

Thanksgiving Done My Way

PUMPKIN SPICE

Anyone who's lived in the United States for any amount of time usually ends up adopting what is probably America's favorite holiday, Thanksgiving. The scent that for me evokes Thanksgiving the most is, of course, pumpkin spice. Pumpkin spice is an American spice blend that, when you smell it, immediately makes you feel that's it's autumn and almost winter.

In the United States you'll find it on the shelves of any supermarket (and in every possible form of drink or food), but of course in Israel we don't have that mix. So I decided to prepare it at home, and its super simple to make! Add a spoonful to coffee with milk, or café au lait, to a slice of baked pumpkin, or to anything that you want to add the scent of autumn. Pumpkin spice contains cinnamon, ginger, nutmeg, and cloves, and although you can easily purchase a readymade spice mix, nothing beats a homemade version, especially since it's so simple to make.

Makes 1 small spice jar

Place 3 Tbs each of ground cinnamon, ground ginger, ground nutmeg, and ground cloves in the jar, seal and shake well.

SPICED PUMPKIN SPREAD

This vegan pumpkin spread is a sort of hybrid between a jam and a nut butter, and it is utterly delicious. You can spread it on your morning toast or pastry, use it as a filling for sweet and savory baked goods, or add it to chicken and beef dishes and stews. So I really recommend preparing this spread and having it on hand.

2.2 lb. (1 kg) pumpkin, with the skin on, washed

Pumpkin Puree

1. Preheat the oven to 180 °C (350 °F) and line a baking tray with parchment paper.

2. Cut the pumpkin into 3–4 large chunks and place in the baking tray and roast until soft.

3. Scoop out the soft flesh into the bowl of a food processor and blend to a smooth puree. Cool to room temperature.

4. The puree will keep for several days in the refrigerator or 3 months in the freezer, stored in an airtight container.

Makes 2.2 lb (1 kg) spread

–

- 2 cups (425 grams) pumpkin puree (see recipe above)
- ¼ cup minus 2 tsp (50 ml) apple cider (or juice)
- ⅓ cup + 1 Tbs (100 ml) maple syrup
- ½ Tbs vanilla extract
- 1 Tbs pumpkin spice (*see recipe on previous page*)
- ½ tsp ground cinnamon
- ¼ tsp salt

Pumpkin Spread

1. Place all of the ingredients in a pot over a low-medium heat, cover partially, and bring to a gentle boil, stirring occasionally. The mixture is very thick and can burn easily, so make sure to keep an eye on it.

2. Reduce to a low heat and cook for 1 hour, until the puree is reduced to ¾ of its original volume. Remove from the heat and cool. The spread will thicken further as it cools down.

3. Transfer to a jar or an airtight container. The spread will keep refrigerated for a month.

CORNBREAD THAT GOES WITH EVERYTHING

People love to eat cornbread pretty much anywhere in the world and at any time of the year, and it's always a nice addition to your table.

Makes 2 loaves or 24 muffins

–

For the dough

1 cup + 2 Tbs (225 grams) sugar

2 1/3 cups (335 grams) all-purpose flour

3/4 cup + 1 Tbs (85 grams) cornmeal

2 Tbs (20 grams) baking powder

1 tsp salt

3 eggs

1/3 cup + 1 Tbs (100 ml) milk

3/4 cup (180 ml) buttermilk

3/4 cup (150 grams) neutral vegetable oil

1. Preheat the oven to 180 °C (350 °F). Grease and line 2 loaf pans with parchment paper (or, if using muffin pans, line with paper baking cups).

2. Place the sugar, flour, cornmeal, baking powder, and salt in a bowl and mix well.

3. Add the eggs, milk, buttermilk, and oil, and mix until just combined (don't overmix).

4. Divide the batter between the pans and bake 25–30 minutes. The cornbread is ready when a toothpick inserted in the center comes out dry.

5. If you're baking the cornbread in a muffin pan, reduce baking time to 15–20 minutes.
Cool on a wire rack.

CORNBREAD TEXAS-STYLE (SAVORY)

For a Texas-style savory cornbread, reduce the amount of sugar to 1/4 cup, and add 1 cup of **sweetcorn kernels (fresh or frozen)**, and **1 diced red bell pepper** or **chopped jalapeño peppers**, to taste.

PUMPKIN SPICE LAYER CAKE WITH MASCARPONE CREAM

As the Jewish year ends, most of the Northern Hemisphere begins its embrace of autumn; sidewalks become decorated with foliage, and the crisp cold air signals the coming of winter, and sometimes even snow.

Meanwhile in Tel Aviv, it's still 27 °C (that's 80 °F!) in the shade, the beaches are full of bathers, and it feels like summer is never going to end. Oh well, autumn will make it here at some point, even if I have to wait another month. In the meantime, it's peak season for the pumpkin family, and I've decided to share one of my favorite autumn recipes, one that's truly festive.

When it comes to pumpkin, we've already talked about how to make pumpkin puree (*see recipe on page 107*) and mouth-watering pumpkin scones (*page 88*), and now it's time for something that you can make for a birthday, a holiday, or for a special occasion, when you want to show off (a bit). This is a layer cake (the non-threatening kind), with layers of aromatic pumpkin, moist and soft. And between the layers, and topping the cake, you have a rich mascarpone cream that lightens the flavor of the pumpkin. You can serve this cake without the cream, but I think the entire recipe creates a cake that's unique and special and perfect for your next dinner.

Makes one 22–24-cm (9–10-in) springform pan

–

For the cake batter

14 Tbs (200 grams) butter at room temperature

1½ cups (300 grams) sugar

A pinch of salt

About 1 cup (200 grams) pumpkin puree (*see recipe on page 107*)

4 eggs

1 brick (250 grams) cream cheese (or ricotta)

7 oz (200 grams) sour cream

1 Tbs pumpkin spice (*see recipe on page 106*)

3 cups (420 grams) all-purpose flour

2 ½ tsp (10 grams) baking powder

–

For the mascarpone cream

About 2 cups (500 grams) mascarpone cheese

1 ½ cups (360 ml) heavy whipping cream

1 Tbs powdered sugar

1. Preheat the oven to 180 °C (350 °F).

2. **Prepare the cake pan:** Grease the pan lightly with canned oil spray or a little butter. Next, cut a circle of baking paper and place in the bottom, and then cut a long strip of baking paper and place it along the inside wall of the pan.

3. Place the butter, sugar, salt, and pumpkin puree in the bowl of a stand mixer fitted with the paddle attachment, and beat to a fluffy, pale, creamy mixture the texture of mayonnaise.

4. Add the eggs one at a time, beating after each addition until the egg is incorporated.

5. Add the cream cheese, sour cream, and pumpkin spice and mix well.

6. Add the flour and baking powder, and mix until just combined (don't overmix).

7. Pour the batter into the cake pan and smooth the top with a spatula.

8. Bake for 45 minutes, until a toothpick inserted in the center of the cake comes out covered with a few moist crumbs. Remove from the oven and cool to room temperature.

9. **Prepare the mascarpone cream:** Place all of the ingredients in the bowl of a stand mixer and whip to a fluffy, thick cream.

10. Release the cake from the pan and, using a bread knife, slice the cake in half horizontally into 2 equal circles.

11. Place the bottom cake layer on a serving plate. Spread half of the mascarpone cream in an even layer and cover with the top cake layer. Spread the remaining mascarpone cream on top, using the back of a spoon to create swirls in the cream. Keep refrigerated until ready to serve.

The holiday of Purim, which commemorates how the Persian-Jewish queen, Esther, saved all of the Jews of Persia from being killed by Haman, an Achaemenid Persian Empire official, is the Jewish equivalent of Halloween. The holiday is celebrated by dressing up in costumes, eating triangular pastries called *hamantaschen*, and drinking wine (in Judaism a significant part of holidays includes drinking ceremonial wine; in Purim, in fact, we're encouraged to drink until senseless). In Israel, these pastries are called Haman's ears; however, the name hamantaschen comes from the German triangle shaped cookies called *omentashen*. Hamantaschen, in fact, means "deep pockets," since Haman the Terrible, who wanted to kill all the Jews of Persia, was very wealthy and thus had "deep pockets" of money.

Now, as a child, I wasn't a huge fan of hamantaschen, for several reasons. First, when you bite into this pastry, you think the dark filling that's peeping out of the top is chocolate—only to discover that it's ground poppy seed or dates (what a disappointment!). And the dough is usually so dry it almost makes you choke. (In Hebrew there's a name for cookies like that: "choking cookies.") Anyone who follows me on Instagram knows how I feel about hamantaschen because whenever Purim rolls around, I remind them just how much I don't like this pastry, at least not in the way it's sold in many places.

However, the recipes I've included in this section are really tasty, and I really like them and eat them myself. My hamantaschen are different because I have sa savory variation, which uses a home-made puff-pastry dough; and also because I have my own hamantaschen dough, which is soft and a far cry from the "choking cookie" dough. An interesting thing about these hamantaschen—they become better with time. I store them in a closed container, and after a few days, the hamantaschen become even softer, which is really cool. In addition, the fillings I use are very different from traditional hamantaschen fillings. For example, I use chocolate espresso, which I call "chocolate for adults," because it's not that sweet and is suited for a more sophisticated, adult palate (*see recipe on page 119*); and pistachio filling, which I love (*see page 118*). By the way, the reason I decided to include hamantaschen in this book was because when we sat down to plan the book, I served my pistachio hamantaschen to the team, and they were blown away, to the point where when I prepared my list of recipes, they asked me why the recipe wasn't there. So here it is.

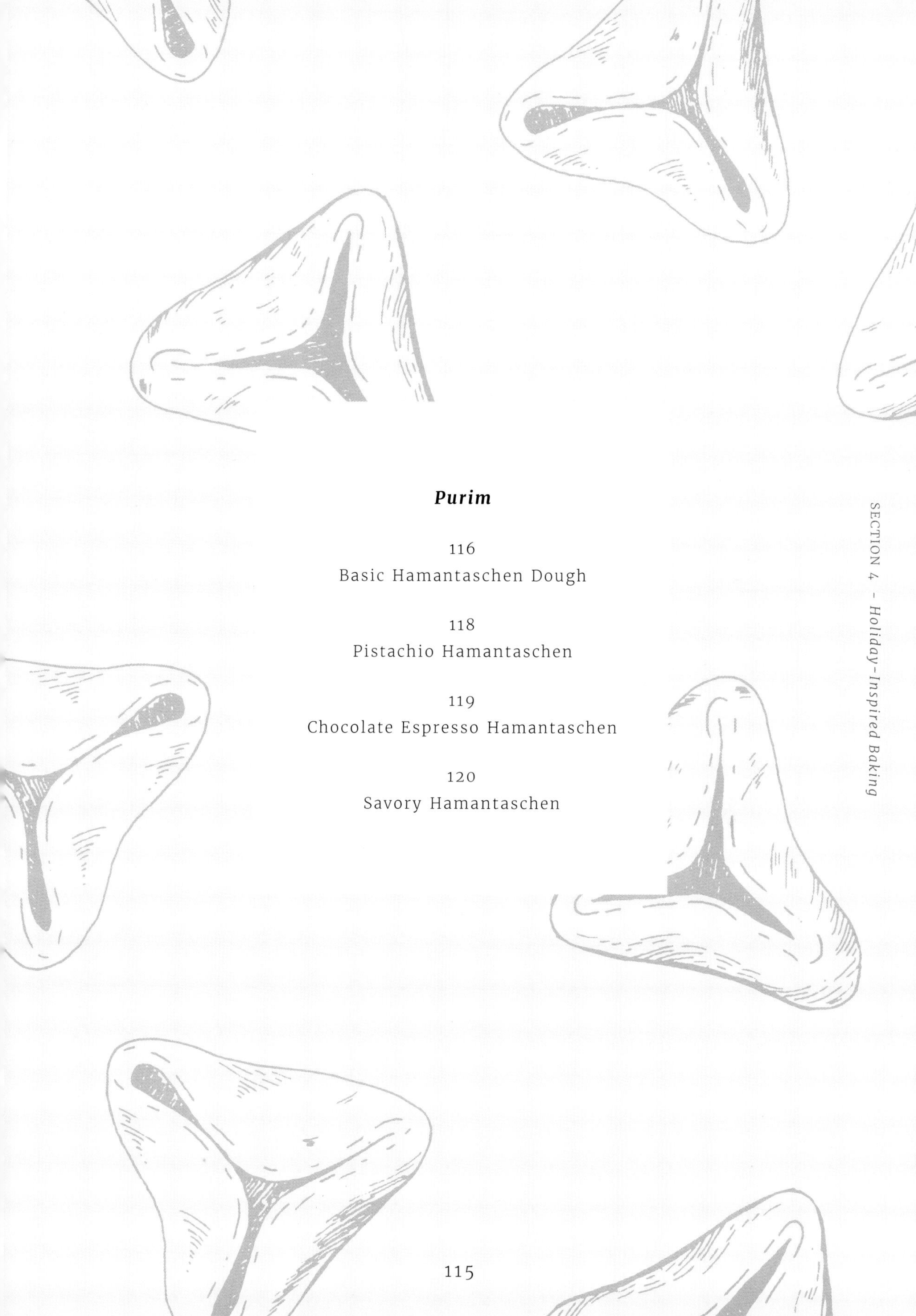

Purim

BASIC HAMANTASCHEN DOUGH

Makes 14–16 pastries

-

1 cup (230 grams) butter, at room temperature

¾ cup (100 grams) powdered sugar

¼ cup (50 grams) sugar

1 egg

1 egg yolk

A pinch of salt

2 ¾ cups + 1 Tbs (400 grams) all-purpose flour

½ cup (50 grams) almond meal

1. Place the butter, powdered sugar, and sugar in the bowl of a stand mixer fitted with the paddle attachment and mix to a pale, fluffy cream.

2. Add the egg and egg yolk one at a time, beating after each addition until fully incorporated.

3. Add the salt, flour, and almond meal, and mix until the dough comes together (don't overmix).

4. Roll into a ball, flatten to a disc, and cover in plastic wrap. Refrigerate overnight or at least 1 hour (the dough can also be frozen).

5. Roll out the dough over a lightly floured surface to a thickness of about 3 mm (0.1 in). Using a cookie cutter, cut into 8-10-cm (3-4-in) circles. Place on a baking tray lined with parchment paper. Refrigerate until ready to use.

A Baker's Tip

I like to use a pastry bag because it's convenient, and I can add the filling in a way that creates uniform pastries; however, you can also work with a tablespoon or teaspoon when adding the filling.

Pistachio Hamantaschen *(page 118)*

Chocolate Espresso Hamantaschen *(page 119)*

PISTACHIO HAMANTASCHEN

Makes 14–16 hamantaschen

–

Basic hamantaschen dough (*see recipe on page 116*)

1 beaten egg, for brushing

–

For the filling

1 cup (100 grams) pistachios, ground

½ cup (100 grams) butter, at room temperature

½ cup (100 grams) sugar

1 egg

3 Tbs (30 grams) cornstarch

2.5 oz (70 grams) pistachio paste (available online and in specialty shops)

A pinch of salt

–

For the topping

Ground pistachios

Powdered sugar

1. **Prepare the filling:** Place all of the ingredients in a bowl and mix to a smooth paste. Transfer to a piping bag, which will make filling the hamantaschen easier.

2. **Assemble the hamantaschen:** Brush the edges of the dough rounds with the beaten egg.

3. Pipe a teaspoon of the filling in the center of each round and fold the sides to make a triangle, pinching gently to seal the hamantaschen. Sprinkle ground pistachios on top and refrigerate for 20 minutes.

4. Preheat the oven to 190 °C (375 °F).

5. Bake for 15–20 minutes, until golden. Cool on a wire rack.

6. Before serving, dust a little powdered sugar on top.

CHOCOLATE ESPRESSO HAMANTASCHEN

Makes 14–16 hamantaschen

–

Basic hamantaschen dough (*see recipe on page 116*)

1 beaten egg, for brushing

–

For the filling

1 ½ cups (250 grams) dark chocolate with a minimum of 60% cocoa solids, chopped

⅓ cup (80 ml) heavy cream

A pinch of salt

1 shot of espresso or 1 tsp instant coffee granules

–

For the topping

Coffee beans, chopped

Coarse sea salt

1. **Prepare the filling:** Place the chopped chocolate in a heat-proof bowl.

2. Bring the heavy cream and salt to a gentle simmer. Pour over the chocolate and let stand for 1 minute before mixing well to a smooth, shiny cream. Add the espresso shot (or instant coffee granules) and mix well.

3. Transfer to a piping bag, and let cool to room temperature.

4. **Assemble the hamantaschen:** Brush the edges of the dough rounds with the beaten egg.

5. Pipe a teaspoon of the filling in the center of each round and fold the sides to make a triangle, pinching gently to seal. Sprinkle chopped coffee beans on each hamantasch and refrigerate for 20 minutes.

6. Preheat the oven to 190 °C (375 °F).

7. Bake for 15–20 minutes, until golden. Cool on a wire rack.

8. Before serving, sprinkle a few flakes of salt on each hamantasch.

SAVORY HAMANTASCHEN

Makes 8–10 hamantaschen

–

For the puff pastry

1 3/4 cup (250 grams) all-purpose flour

1 tsp salt

1/4 cup (50 grams) butter, softened

1/2 cup (120 ml) cold water

2/3 cup (150 grams) butter, cut into small cubes and frozen for several minutes

Or

500 grams (1 lb) store-bought all-butter puff pastry, thawed

–

For the cheese filling

1 cup (250 grams) ricotta cheese

4 Tbs Parmesan cheese, grated

1/2 tsp ground black pepper

1/4 tsp salt

–

For the sweet potato filling

Cheese filling (see recipe above)

2 sweet potatoes or purple yams, peeled and cut into 1–2-cm (0.4–0.8-in) cubes

Extra virgin olive oil

Sea salt

For the grilled eggplant filling

Cheese filling (see recipe above)

1/2 eggplant, sliced in 5-mm (0.2-in) rounds

Extra virgin olive oil

Sea salt

–

For the topping

1 beaten egg, for brushing

White and black sesame seeds

1. **Prepare the puff pastry:** Place the flour, salt, and softened butter in the bowl of a stand mixer fitted with the paddle attachment and mix to a crumbly mixture.

2. Pour the water while mixing continuously, and knead just until a dough forms and pulls away from the sides of the bowl. Add the water gradually, as you may not need to use all of it.

3. Add the frozen butter cubes and mix just until they're incorporated into the dough but the chunks are still visible. Make sure not to overwork the dough.

4. Shape the dough into a 15-cm (6-in) rectangle, cover in plastic wrap, and refrigerate for at least 30 minutes.

5. Place the dough on a lightly floured worksurface and roll into a rectangle that's 5 mm (0.2 in) thick. Fold the bottom towards the center, then fold the left side towards the center. Fold the top toward the bottom. The dough should look like a closed book with a total of 4 layers.

→

6. Roll out the dough to a 15x30-cm (6×12-in) rectangle, 5 mm (0.2 in) thick, and repeat the book folds in step 5. Cover with plastic wrap and refrigerate for 30 minutes.

7. Repeat 2 more times, for a total of 6 book folds.

8. Chill the dough for at least 30 minutes prior to using. Alternatively, the dough can be kept in the freezer, tightly wrapped, until ready to use.

9. **Prepare the cheese filling:** Place all of the ingredients in a bowl and mix to a smooth cream. Transfer to a piping bag and keep refrigerated until ready to use.

10. **Prepare the sweet potato filling:** Preheat the oven to 180 °C (350 °F) and line a baking tray with parchment paper.

11. Place the sweet potato cubes in the tray, drizzle a little olive oil, and sprinkle salt. Toss to coat and roast in the oven for about 30 minutes, until the sweet potatoes are soft. Cool to room temperature.

12. Mash the sweet potato to a smooth puree and add to the cheese filling. Taste and adjust the seasoning to your taste. Transfer to a piping bag and keep refrigerated until ready to use.

13. **Prepare the grilled eggplant filling:** Preheat the oven to 180 °C (350 °F) and line a baking tray with parchment paper.

14. Place the eggplant rounds in the tray, drizzle a little olive oil and sprinkle salt. Toss to coat and roast in the oven for about 20-25 minutes, until the eggplant is golden brown. Cool to room temperature.

15. Finely chop the grilled eggplants and add to the cheese filling. Taste and adjust the seasoning to your taste. Transfer to a piping bag and keep refrigerated until ready to use.

→

→

16. **Assemble the hamantaschen:** Roll out the puff pastry over a lightly floured surface to a thickness of about 3 mm (0.1 in). Cut 10-cm (4-in) rounds using a cookie cutter.

17. Brush the edges of the rounds with a thin coat of the beaten egg.

18. Pipe a teaspoon of the filling in the center of each round and fold the sides to make a triangle, pinching gently to seal the hamantaschen. Transfer to the baking tray lined with parchment paper and refrigerate for 30 minutes.

19. Preheat the oven to 200 °C (400 °F).

20. Brush the hamantaschen with the beaten egg and sprinkle sesame seeds on top.

21. Bake for 10 minutes before reducing the oven temperature to 180 °C (350 °F). Bake for an additional 10 minutes, until golden and puffed. Cool on a wire rack.

Sweet Potato Filling
(page 120)
Savory Hamantaschen
with Cheese Filling
(page 120)

Grilled Eggplant Filling
(page 120)

Shavuot (also known as The Feast of Weeks) is the festival celebrated on the fiftieth day after Passover. In Israel, you could simply rename this holiday “the pastry chef holiday,” because the tradition for this holiday is to consume a lot of dairy dishes, especially cheesecakes. While there are various explanations for this, they don’t really explain how Shavuot became the cheesecake holiday. The truth is, one of the major dairy manufacturers in Israel probably said to themselves, many years ago, "Why not turn this into a celebration of dairy dishes—cheeses, milk, and cream?" So they did. And now Shavuot is our—the pastry chefs'—holiday, and you’re going to love it.

While you’ll find a lot of dairy dishes served during Shavuot, some of them very traditional (like my mom’s Çukur, which you can find on page 139), the classic cake that nearly all bakeries and pastry chefs make on Shavuot is cheesecake.
I make a New York cheesecake: I mean, how can you resist a perfect, classic New York cheesecake? One year, on Shavuot, I made this cheesecake and brought it to my family meal. Luckily for me, not all of the cake was eaten, so naturally, I took it home (I mean, cheesecake, you think I’m going to leave that behind?). So we were walking to my mom’s car, since she was going to drive me to my apartment, when disaster struck.

You know that episode in the series *Friends*, when Chandler got a cheesecake delivered to him by mistake (it was Mrs. Braverman's cheesecake), and then, during an argument over who was supposed to eat it, Rachel dropped the cake in the middle of the hallway? Well, that’s what happened to me. This incredible, delicious piece of cheesecake slipped out of my mom’s hand and right onto the middle of the road. And I was **so** disappointed!

So I did what any normal person would do: I bent down, picked it up, and threw it away (and you thought I was going to eat it off the road with a fork like Joey, Chandler, and Rachel did, didn’t you?). Oh well, maybe it was for the best, but it was a real tragedy because there’s nothing like a New York cheesecake.

Shavuot
(The Feast of Weeks)

CLASSIC NEW YORK CHEESECAKE

Cheesecake is considered very much a Jewish American dish. I mean, New York cheesecake, right? But did you know that cheesecake has been around for nearly 3,000 years, and its source is Ancient Greece? According to John Segreto, author of *Cheesecake Madness* (Simon & Schuster, 1984), athletes would eat the cake to boost their energy (while today's marathon runners fill up on pasta), and it was also served at the weddings of wealthy Greeks.

During the Roman Empire, cheesecake also spread to the masses. While it's not clear when Jews first embraced cheesecake (it might have been during the Greek occupation of Judea or during the Roman era a century or so later), the Jewish people loved cheesecake and soon adapted it to their local tastes and ingredients.

Makes one 20-cm (8-in) springform pan

-

For the base

1 1/2-2 cups ground graham crackers, speculoos, or petit beurre shortbread cookies

3 Tbs (40 grams) cold butter

-

For the cheesecake

1 cup (200 grams) sugar

1 1/2 lb (670 grams) cream cheese

1/3 cup (70 grams) sour cream

4 eggs

1/2 cup (120 grams) heavy cream

1 1/2 tsp vanilla extract

1/2 tsp salt

-

For the sour cream topping:

3/4 cup (200 grams) sour cream

4 Tbs (40 grams) powdered sugar

1. **The day before:** Grease and line a springform pan with parchment paper.

2. Place the crackers or cookies and the butter in the bowl of a food processor and blend to a mixture resembling wet sand.

3. Transfer the mixture to the pan and press evenly to the base. Freeze for 20 minutes.

4. **Prepare the cheesecake filling:** Place a roasting pan filled with water at the bottom of the oven to create a humid environment, and preheat the oven to 150 °C (300 °F).

5. Place all of the cheesecake ingredients in a blender or food processor and blend until the batter is very smooth and resembles pudding.

6. Pour the batter over the crust and bake for 30 minutes.

7. Remove from the oven and cool the cake to room temperature before covering with plastic wrap and refrigerating overnight.

8. **The next day:** Release the cake from the pan and place on a serving plate.

9. **Prepare the sour cream topping:** Mix the sour cream and powdered sugar until smooth, and spread over the cheesecake evenly. The cake will keep refrigerated for several days.

For a very cool, unique variation on this classic cheesecake, check out the Brie cheesecake recipe on page 217.

To Quiche or Not to Quiche?

A basic quiche recipe is quite simple—and yet also quite easy to ruin. I noticed this myself in situations where I've eaten a quiche and had that feeling that it was off, not quite there, not quite a quiche. So what is a quiche? Well, a quiche has a dough shell base, usually neutral, and it's filled with vegetables and cheese or some other combination, and *crème royale*—and that's what makes it a quiche.

A casserole isn't a quiche, and quiche also isn't a quick dinner you just throw together into a pan. It's more refined, and has more texture, and what goes into the quiche itself requires more thought than a simple casserole. I think that the understanding of the more complex nature of quiches has become even more obvious to me because of the brunches I host. At my brunches, one of the recipes is usually a quiche, not only because it makes sense for me to make it but also because it's a classic dish and delicious when done right! My first quiche recipe was a mushroom quiche, and everyone seemed to love that one the most. In fact, that's the recipe I've been asked for the most, but I didn't just want to give the recipe away for this one. Instead, I created a workshop, usually for private groups or around Shavuot, and the participants get the recipe. Along the way I realized that I also wanted to save the recipe for this book.

Like with tarts, people tend to shy away from making a dish when it requires more than one step—but quiche is simple and you can make the dough or the base and freeze it, and then make the filling. It's not a big deal, but it does require precision; the result should be creamy, not bland, flaky, and not wet—with a perfect balance between the base and filling. Something you want more of—not something that gets left on the plate.

BASIC QUICHE CRUST AND *CRÈME ROYALE*

Makes one 20-cm (8-in) tart pan

-

1 ¾ cups (250 grams) cake flour

½ tsp salt

½ Tbs sugar

½ cup (125 grams) cold butter, cut into cubes

¾ cup (180 ml) cold water

Basic Quiche Crust

1. Place the cake flour, salt, sugar, and butter in the bowl of a stand mixer fitted with the paddle attachment and mix to a mixture that resembles coarse meal, with a few pea-sized pieces of butter remaining.

2. Add the water gradually and while continuously beating, 1 tablespoon of cold water at a time, and mix until a dough just forms. You may not need to use all of the water.

3. Roll into a ball, flatten to a disc, and cover in plastic wrap. Refrigerate for at least 1 hour. The dough can also be frozen for up to 3 months, tightly wrapped.

4. Place the dough between two sheets of parchment paper and roll into a 24-cm (10-in) circle. Transfer to the pan and press to the bottom and sides. Place in the freezer until ready to use.

2 eggs

½ cup (125 ml) whole milk

½ cup (125 ml) heavy cream

½ tsp salt

½ tsp ground black pepper

A pinch of ground nutmeg

Crème Royale

1. Place the eggs, milk, heavy cream, salt, pepper, and nutmeg in a bowl and mix well.

PURPLE SWEET POTATO AND GOAT CHEESE QUICHE

- 1 basic quiche crust (*see recipe on page 131*)
- *Crème royale* (*see recipe on page 131*)
- 4 cups (600 grams) purple yams or sweet potato, cut into 1–2-cm (0.4-in) sticks, with the peel
- Sea salt
- Extra virgin olive oil
- 3.5 oz (100 grams) goat cheese, cut into 5-mm (0.2-in) rounds
- ½ cup (50 grams) Parmesan cheese, grated

1. Preheat the oven to 180 °C (350 °F) and line a baking tray with parchment paper.

2. Place the sweet potato sticks on the tray, drizzle olive oil, sprinkle a little sea salt, and toss to coat. Roast 20-30 minutes, until golden and crispy. Cool to room temperature.

3. Spread the sweet potato sticks over the crust evenly and place the goat cheese rounds on top to cover.

4. Sprinkle the grated Parmesan on top.

5. Pour the *crème royale* almost to the edge of the crust.

6. Bake for 45–50 minutes, until the quiche is golden and baked through.

Variation

Feel free to substitute the sweet potato with pumpkin.

MUSHROOM QUICHE

1 basic quiche crust (*see recipe on page 131*)
Crème royale (*see recipe on page 131*)
2 Tbs (30 grams) butter
4–5 cups (500–600 grams) assorted mushrooms, sliced and stems trimmed
Salt, to taste
½ cup (50 grams) Parmesan cheese, grated

1. Melt the butter in a frying pan. Add the mushrooms and fry until softened. Season with salt and let cool to room temperature.

2. Preheat the oven to 180 °C (350 °F).

3. Spread the sautéed mushrooms over the crust evenly.

4. Sprinkle the grated Parmesan on top.

5. Pour the *crème royale* over the vegetables, almost to the edge of the crust.

6. Bake for 45–50 minutes, until the quiche is golden and baked through.

EGGPLANT AND ARTICHOKE QUICHE

- 1 basic quiche crust (*see recipe on page 131*)
- *Crème royale* (*see recipe on page 131*)
- 1 small eggplant, halved lengthwise and sliced, or cut into 2 ½-cm (1-in) cubes
- Sea salt
- Extra virgin olive oil
- 10.5 oz (300 grams) jarred grilled artichokes in olive oil, strained
- ½ cup (50 grams) Parmesan cheese, grated

1. Preheat the oven to 180 °C (350 °F) and line a baking tray with parchment paper.

2. Place the sliced or diced eggplant on the tray, drizzle olive oil, sprinkle a little sea salt, and toss to coat. Roast until golden brown and tender, about 30 minutes. Cool to room temperature.

3. Spread the roasted eggplant and grilled artichokes over the crust evenly.

4. Sprinkle the grated Parmesan on top.

5. Pour the *crème royale* almost to the edge of the crust.

6. Bake for 45–50 minutes, until the quiche is golden and baked through.

CHEESE BOUREKAS

There are many theories about the origin of bourekas. Börek are of Ottoman origin and are a family of baked, stuffed pastries that are made of a thin flaky dough. The bourekas were brought to Israel by the Sephardic Jews who came from the Balkan countries, which include Bulgaria, Turkey, and North Africa. Bourekas are usually made out of puff pastry and filled with various savory fillings, such as feta cheese, kashkaval cheese, and more.

Bourekas are another one of the recipes that are part of my heritage, since you'll find this pastry throughout the Balkan countries.

I remember that once, when I was little, I went to visit Savta Vicki with my mom or my brother; we decided to surprise her and not tell her we were coming. So when when she saw us, she became a bit flustered, exclaiming, "Why didn't you warn me you were coming? I would have prepared food!" A second later, she must have felt so embarrassed that she went into the kitchen and I followed her. She handed me a plate, opened the oven, and put a bourekas on the plate. Next, she opened the pot on the stovetop and put a stuffed pepper on the plate; then she opened the refrigerator and pulled out a cheese the Bulgarians call cirne (like feta cheese), and placed that on the plate. Finally, she turned to me and said, "Next time tell me when you're coming—I'll make food!" I remember thinking, "If that's not food, what is considered food?"

Makes 10–14 pastries

-

Homemade puff pastry (*see Savory Hamantaschen recipe on page 120)* or 500 grams (about 1 lb) store-bought all-butter puff pastry, thawed

-

For the cheese filling

½ brick (125 grams) cream cheese

4.4 oz (125 grams) feta cheese, crumbled

2 Tbs grated Parmesan cheese

-

For the topping

1 beaten egg

Black and white sesame seeds

1. **Prepare the cheese filling:** Place all of the ingredients in a bowl and mix to a smooth cream. Transfer to a piping bag.

2. **Assemble the bourekas:** Preheat the oven to 190 °C (375 °F) and line a baking tray with parchment paper.

3. Roll the puff pastry over a lightly floured surface until it's 5 mm (0.2 in) thick. Using a sharp knife, cut into 6-10-cm (2.5-4-in) rectangles.

4. Brush the edges with the beaten egg. Pipe about a tablespoon of the cheese filling in the center of each rectangle and fold into a triangle, lightly pressing the edges to seal. Transfer to the baking tray.

5. Brush the bourekas with the beaten egg and sprinkle black and white sesame seeds on top.

6. Bake for 30 minutes, until the bourekas are puffed and golden.

For as long as I can remember, our family table, especially on Shavuot and often on Shabbat, has always included my mom's Çukur: a huge, spiral-shaped pastry made of puff pastry and filled with cheese and spinach. My mom learned to make Çukur from her mother-in-law, my Savta Victoria, whom we called Savta Vicki. I think it's really wonderful that my mom chose to preserve her mother-in-law's recipes and traditions, in addition to her own mother's, and that approach is just one of the many qualities I admire in my mom.

The Çukur my mom makes has the best taste, but I remember something interesting about it: The center was always a bit under-baked. I think that was a great part of the recipe—that the outside was flaky and the inside a bit less. So remember that it's quite okay to eat a pastry that's a bit under-baked.

Even before I decided to write this book, maybe even before I became a professional pastry chef, I knew that I was going to include this recipe for Çukur in a book. Initially, I'd thought about a book that would have recipes that were both my mom's and mine, and in this case, the difference would have been my addition of a puff pastry made from scratch (my mom uses readymade puff pastry). This would have been a melding of our baking hands, where we both add our unique touches to this wonderful family recipe. Therefore, this Çukur recipe is a combination of both our worlds—my mom's and mine—and I know it's a recipe that should be passed down through generations. This recipe to me truly symbolizes what it means to have a "family recipe." You can serve this dish on any occasion or save it for a special one, such as a holiday meal.

ÇUKUR*
(A HUGE SPIRAL-SHAPED BOUREKAS FILLED WITH CHEESE AND SPINACH)

*Pronounced *chu'kur*

Makes one large pastry

-

Homemade puff pastry (*see Savory Hamantaschen recipe on page 120*) or 500 grams (about 1 lb) store-bought all-butter puff pastry, thawed

-

For the cheese and spinach filling

1 Tbs butter

1 bunch flat leaf spinach, washed

1 brick (250 grams) cream cheese

2 Tbs mascarpone cheese

9 oz (250 grams) Bulgarian style feta cheese, crumbled

1 cup (100 grams) kashkaval (or any semi-hard sheep's milk cheese), grated

1 Tbs all-purpose flour

½ Tbs ground black pepper

-

For the topping

2–3 Tbs melted butter

2 Tbs white sesame seeds

-

To serve

Hard-boiled eggs

1. Remove the spinach stems and separate the leaves.

2. Melt the butter in a frying pan. Add the spinach leaves and sauté until wilted and soft. Cool.

3. Place the spinach leaves in a bowl and add the cream cheese, mascarpone, Bulgarian style feta, kashkaval cheese, flour, and black pepper. Mix well. If the filling is too salty, add a few teaspoons of heavy cream.

4. Preheat the oven to 190 °C (375 °F) and line a baking tray with parchment paper.

5. Roll the puff pastry over a lightly floured surface to a 20×40-cm (8x16-in) rectangle, 5 mm (0.2 in) thick. Cut in half lengthwise, so that you end up with 2 rectangles, each 10×40 cm (4×16 in).

6. Brush a rectangle with the beaten egg and spread half of the cheese-spinach filling evenly. Tightly roll into a roulade and then roll into a spiral. Place in the baking tray. Follow the same steps to create another roulade with the remaining puff pastry rectangle and filling. Attach the end of the roulade to the end of the spiral, and continue to form one large spiral.

7. Brush the pastry with the melted butter and sprinkle sesame seeds on top.

8. Bake for 40–60 minutes, until baked through, puffed and golden.

9. Slice and serve with a hard-boiled egg.

Section 5

Fika (Coffee Break)

Hygge and Fika

Despite the fact that they live for several months of the year in near dark, the Scandinavians are considered the happiest people in the world, so it's no wonder that these are the people who brought us the lovely-sounding words *Hygge* (in Danish the philosophy of being happy) and *Fika* (coffee break). Fika essentially means giving myself the time to do the things that make me happy!

A few years ago, Uri (my significant other) brought me two coffee saucers and a tray from Stockholm that have the word "Fika" printed on them, and I loved them. A few months ago, I did a live Instagram video where I taught how to make kanelbullar (yes, of course the recipe is in this book; see page 144). When I finished, I sliced the kanelbullar and placed them on the Fika dishes Uri had brought me.

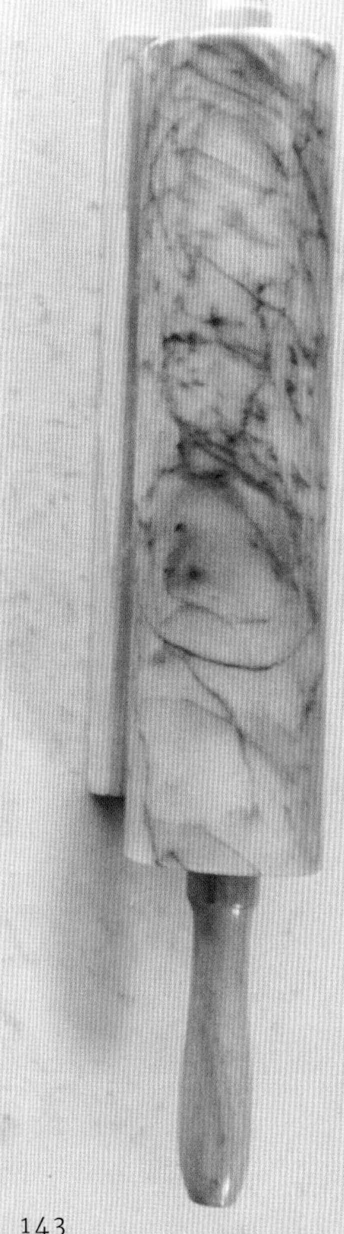

One of my followers then wrote to me to point out that the logo of another bakery appeared in the photo (there's a local Swedish bakery in Tel Aviv called Fika), and did I know that? So I explained the meaning of Fika and why I used those dishes. Today our world has become so global that people are familiar with dishes like kanelbullar, but unfortunately, they still don't know what Fika means: Fika isn't just a logo, it's a state of mind, and one that I really relate to. The Scandinavians truly know how to live a life of happiness, to live a life of carpe diem. And I also try to sieze the day, to allow myself the pleasure of the time to sit and have coffee with the people I love. In my life and in my book, Fika has an important role. Indeed, it has a place of honor.

KANELBULLAR*
SWEDISH CARDAMOM AND CINNAMON BUNS

*Pronounced *cannelbola*

During my internship at Noma, we worked five days a week in 18-hour shifts. Coming from Israel, where most restaurants work seven days a week and the chefs work six days a week, I thought, "Wow, what a luxury, working only five days a week—I'll have so much time to do things!" Boy was I wrong! One of the hardest things of our work day in Noma was that it started really early in the morning, hours before any bakery or café was open, so that I couldn't even get a coffee or a bite to eat before starting my shift. This meant I would end up having my first cup of good coffee at Noma and then would eat only when the staff had its breakfast or lunch (several hours later).

On my days off, I would go and explore the different bakeries in Copenhagen, to learn about the pastries they made. I wanted either to try something new every time, or to try the same thing at different bakeries; and you know what? No matter where I ate or what I tried—it was always different, always unique. Now, you'd think I would have packed on the weight with all those pastries, but we worked so hard at Noma, physical hard work, that I didn't gain a pound, and I managed to burn off all of the calories from those incredible pastries.

I remember that there were a number of bakeries on the street near my apartment, and indeed, Copenhagen has bakeries on pretty much every block and street, which is really fun. Every bakery has a huge selection of pastries, many of which are made with cinnamon and vanilla—it's such an incredible experience. I mean, you can walk into a bakery and choose the simplest pastry and it's still delicious!

And that's where I first experienced the kanelbullar. Now, there are many similarities between Danish, Swedish, and other Scandinavian pastries, and there are a lot of pastries that feature cinnamon and cardamom, which is very Scandinavian, but the kanelbullar itself is Swedish. The kanelbullar is quite popular in Copenhagen, probably because many Swedes work there who live in the city of Malmö, which is just a short drive or train ride away. These Swedes commute to work in Copenhagen on a daily basis, so it's no surprise that there are a lot of Swedish bakeries in Copenhagen. Of course, the flavors that are local to Sweden and Denmark have become intertwined, but this particular pastry is very much a Swedish pastry, and it even has its own holiday, National Kanelbullar Day, which is celebrated on October 4 each year. And the dough? I mean, what a perfect bite! Every time I ate kanelbullar in Copenhagen, it was so soft, so good, that it blew my mind!

I soon began to realize that none of the amazing Scandinavian pastries we were making had yet to make their way to Israel (things have changed slightly since then). I'd always been fascinated by Scandinavian culture and history (not just the classic Hans Christian Andersen stories), even as a child, but I knew almost nothing about their local cuisine.

When I started running my workshops on Danish and Scandinavian pastries, I would ask the participants whether any of them knew how these spices came to be in the pastries. It was during those workshops that I discovered, through an Iraqi sous chef working with me, that Jews of Iraqi descent use cardamom in some of their cookies. From him and from others, I learned that cardamom is added to the traditional Iraqi *kaak,* which is a kind of dry pretzel cookie. Since we know that the Vikings traded all over Europe and as far east as Central Asia, their trading likely introduced them to Indian spices like cardamom and cinnamon, which is probably why you can find them in many of the Scandinavian pastries. And that's one of the great things about food—it helps us to understand how people move from place to place, acquiring new dishes and spices.

→

→

Makes 16–20 buns

–

For the dough

3 tsp (13 grams) active dry yeast (or 3 Tbs (25 grams) fresh yeast)

1 cup (250 ml) whole milk, at room temperature

3 ½ Tbs (40 grams) sugar

⅓ cup (80 grams) butter, melted

4 cups (500 grams) bread flour

A pinch of salt

2 Tbs ground cardamom

1 egg

1 beaten egg, for brushing

–

For the filling

⅔ cup (160 grams) butter, softened

About ⅔ cup (160 grams) sugar

4 Tbs ground cinnamon

2 tsp vanilla extract

1 tsp ground cardamom

2 Tbs flour

–

For the glaze

1 cup (200 grams) sugar

⅓ cup + 4 tsp (100 ml) water

Pearl sugar

–

Baking tray lined with parchment paper

1. **Prepare the dough:** Place the yeast and milk in the bowl of a stand mixer fitted with the dough hook and mix well. Add the sugar and melted butter and mix.

2. Add the salt and ground cardamom to the flour and mix. Gradually and while continuously kneading, add the flour mixture to the mixer. The dough shouldn't be too wet or dry, so you may not need to use all of the flour.

3. Add the egg and knead until the dough separates from the bowl.

4. Transfer the dough to a greased bowl, cover, and let rise for 30 minutes.

5. **Prepare the filling:** Place all of the ingredients in a bowl and mix well. Set aside at room temperature until ready to use. The filling should have a spreadable consistency; if it's too cold it will tear the dough when spread, and if too soft, will melt.

6. **Assemble the buns:** Place the dough on a lightly floured worksurface and roll into a 40×40-cm (16×16-in) rectangle, about 5 mm (0.2 in) thick.

7. Spread an even layer of the filling all the way to the edges.

8. Fold the dough into thirds, as you would fold a letter; grab the top edge and fold it towards the center, and then grab the bottom edge and fold it over to cover.

9. Using a pizza cutter, cut the dough into 1-cm (0.4-in)-wide strips. Stretch and twist each strip several times and coil it into a bun. Place in the tray, cover, and let rise for 25 minutes.

10. Preheat the oven to 180 °C (350 °F).

11. Brush with the beaten egg and bake for 10–15 minutes, until golden.

12. **Meanwhile, prepare the glaze:** Place the sugar and water in a saucepan and bring to a boil. Set aside.

13. Brush the buns with the hot syrup as soon as they come out of the oven and sprinkle pearl sugar on top. Cool on a rack.

Rugelach, which comes from the Yiddish *rogalek*, is a filled pastry that originates in the Jewish communities of Poland. Rugelach is popular in Israel and among Jewish communities throughout Europe and the United States. Traditional rugelach take the form of a crescent, created by rolling a triangle of dough around the filling.

When I lived in the United States, I soon realized that while you can find rugelach in many bakeries, it's not really the kind you find in Israel. Growing up in Israel, I lived near a bakery that sold these tiny rugelach, and the smell they had was divine. They were usually made with chocolate or cinnamon and covered with sugar syrup.

In the United States, the first rugelach I ate was a type of cookie made of cookie dough or short crust pastry filled with cheese or jam. I didn't know if it was this particular place that made them this way, and then I found the same kind of rugelach in all the other bakeries. I asked myself, how is it that the rugelach in the United States and in Israel are so different? But then I realized that there are many pastries that are completely different, depending on where you come from. Still, I feel strongly that the rugelach in Israel are the best in the world and should have made it to the United States (just like the babka made a comeback there). Which is why my rugelach, the one you're about to make, is the Israeli kind.

RUGELACH

Makes 35-40 rugelach

-

Kanelbullar dough (*see recipe on page 146*)

-

For the filling

2/3 cup (160 grams) butter, softened

About 3/4 cup (80 grams) cocoa powder

1 1/3 cups (160 grams) powdered sugar

3.5 oz (100 grams) cookie crumbs

A pinch of salt

1 tsp vanilla extract

1/2 cup Nutella or hazelnut chocolate spread

-

For the syrup

1 cup (200 grams) sugar

1/3 cup + 4 tsp (100 ml) water

-

1 beaten egg, for brushing

1. **Prepare the filling:** Place all of the ingredients in a bowl and mix well. Set aside at room temperature until ready to use. The filling should have a spreadable consistency; if it's too cold it will tear the dough when spread, and if too soft, will melt.

2. **Assemble the rugelach:** Line a baking tray with parchment paper. Place the dough on a lightly floured worksurface and roll into a 40×40-cm (16×16-in) rectangle, about 5 mm (0.2 in) thick.

3. Spread an even layer of the filling all the way to the edges.

4. Fold the dough into thirds, as you would fold a letter; grab the top edge and fold it towards the center, and then grab the bottom edge and fold it over to cover. Roll into a 20×40-cm (8×16-in) rectangle, 5 mm (0.2 in) thick.

5. Using a pizza cutter, cut the dough in half, to 2 long rectangle strips of 10×40 cm (4×16 in). Make a notch every 6 cm (2.5 in) along one side of each strip and use that marking to cut into triangles.

6. Cut a small slit at the wide end of each triangle, then tightly roll up into a crescent shape, making sure the tip is underneath.

7. Place the rugelach in the tray, spaced 4 cm (1.5 in) apart. Cover, let rise for 45-60 minutes.

8. Preheat the oven to 180 °C (350 °F). Brush each crescent with the beaten egg. Bake for 20-25 minutes, until golden brown.

9. **Prepare the syrup:** Place the sugar and water in a saucepan and bring to a boil. Set aside.

10. Brush the rugelach with the hot syrup as soon as they come out of the oven. Cool.

PUMPKIN SPICE CINNAROLL

This is a seasonal take on the classic cinnaroll.

Makes 1 26-cm (10.5-in) square baking pan

–

For the dough

3 3/4 cups + 1 Tbs (540 grams) all-purpose flour

2 tsp (8 grams) active dry yeast

1/4 cup + 2 Tbs (75 grams) sugar

About 2/3 cups (160 grams) pumpkin spread (*see recipe on page 107*)

2 eggs

3 egg yolks

2 tsp salt

1 heaped tsp pumpkin spice, (*see recipe on page 106*)

1/4 cup (60 grams) extra virgin olive oil

1 beaten egg, for brushing

–

For the filling

2 Tbs pumpkin spice (*see recipe on page 106*)

6 Tbs sugar

1/2 tsp salt

5 Tbs pumpkin puree or pumpkin spread (*see recipe on page 107*)

–

For the cream cheese icing

1 brick (250 grams) cream cheese

2 Tbs powdered sugar

1. **Prepare the dough:** Place the flour, active dry yeast, sugar, pumpkin spread, eggs, yolks, salt, and pumpkin spice in the bowl of a stand mixer fitted with the dough hook, and mix on a low speed for 2 minutes, until the dough comes together.

2. Increase the speed slightly and knead for 7 minutes, until you have a soft, smooth dough.

3. Reduce to a low speed, add the olive oil, and knead until it's fully incorporated into the dough.

4. Transfer the dough to a greased bowl, shape into a ball, cover with a towel or a loose plastic wrap, and let rise for 90 minutes, until it doubles in size.

5. **Prepare the filling:** Place the pumpkin spice, sugar, and salt in a bowl and mix well.

6. Place the dough on a lightly floured worksurface and roll into a rectangle 5 mm (0.2 in) thick.

7. Spread an even layer of the pumpkin puree or spread and sprinkle the pumpkin spice mixture on top. Starting with the long side, roll into a tight coil.

8. Line a baking tray with parchment paper. Using the blunt side of the knife, make scores in the coil, dividing it into 3 equal parts. Make scores in each part, dividing each into 3 equal parts and cut. You should end up with 9 equal pieces.

9. Place the rolls in the baking tray, cut side facing up, leaving 5 mm (0.2 in) of space between them.

10. Brush with the beaten egg, and let rise uncovered for 1 hour, until the rolls have risen and filled all the gaps.

11. Preheat the oven to 180 °C (350 °F).

12. Bake for 30 minutes, until the rolls are golden brown. Cool to room temperature.

13. **Prepare the cream cheese icing:** Mix the cream cheese and powdered sugar to a smooth cream. Spread the icing over the rolls.

I Can't Believe It's Tahini

During some of my recent visits to London, it became very clear that the biggest trend to overtake the British kitchen was the Middle Eastern food trend. And this trend, combined with the trend toward healthier food and eating, created fertile ground for pastries that include healthy ingredients, like tahini. And indeed, you'll see the use of tahini in bakeries in England far more than in Israel (where at the most you might find tahini cookies). I make it a point to visit and taste pastries wherever I go—both in Israel and overseas (although I do eat more pastries overseas, I'll admit). In London, in every bakery I walked into, I saw them using tahini, in at least one pastry if not more—often in brownies or cookies.

Which is kind of funny, if you think about it: Here we are, in Israel, where tahini is pretty much a national food, and we barely use it in our baking, when we should be! Instead it's more popular as dip or as a salad dressing, or as a topping on a pita with falafel and salad. Even tahini cookies are rarely sold at bakeries. And there are just so many things you can do with tahini: If I can bake a cake with cashew butter or hazelnut butter, I can easily replace that with raw tahini, which has a similar texture. When I got back to Israel from my last visit to England, I decided to come up with my own recipe that uses tahini, one that would use tahini as a replacement for butter (or other oil) and would include tahini's unique flavor.

So here is my recipe for tahini brownies, with tahini replacing some of the butter. The result is really tasty, and I promise, you won't miss the butter! And they're even kind of healthy. Okay, so I wouldn't eat them **instead** of a salad, but I would definitely recommend them as a dessert.

SPELT BROWNIES WITH TAHINI

Makes one 8-in (20-cm) square brownie pan

-

- 2 2/3 cups (400 grams) dark chocolate with a minimum of 60% cocoa solids, chopped
- 3/4 cup (200 grams) raw tahini + 1/4 cup (50 grams) for drizzling
- 14 Tbs (200 grams) butter at room temperature
- 8 eggs
- 2 1/2 cups (500 grams) sugar
- 1/2 tsp salt
- 1 3/4 cups (220 grams) whole meal spelt flour
- 1/2 cup (70 grams) cocoa powder
- 1 Tbs sea salt

1. Preheat the oven to 170 °C (340 °F) and line a brownie pan with parchment paper.

2. Place the chocolate, 3/4 cup tahini, and butter in a heat-proof bowl over a saucepan of simmering water (or a bain-marie pot) and heat until melted. Stir to a smooth and shiny mixture.

3. Place the sugar, eggs, and 1/2 a teaspoon of salt in the bowl of a stand mixer fitted with the paddle attachment, and mix until pale and fluffy.

4. Reduce the speed and pour the melted chocolate mixture while mixing continuously.

5. Add the spelt flour and cocoa powder, and mix until the mixture is smooth and lump-free (don't overmix).

6. Pour the batter into the brownie pan and smooth the top with a spatula.

7. Drizzle thin streaks of tahini over the brownie batter and use a toothpick to draw over the lines to create swirls.

8. Bake 35-40 minutes, until a toothpick inserted in the center comes out with a few moist crumbs.

9. Sprinkle sea salt on top and let the brownies cool completely in the pan.

10. The brownies will keep for up to 7 days at room temperature if stored in an airtight container, or for s3 months in the freezer.

LOUISE'S AWESOME BROWNIES

When I started my internship at Noma (which, as of writing this book, had been awarded the title "top restaurant in the world" four times), Noma's pastry sous chef, Louise Bannon, was still working there, but not for very long. I'd being following Louise on Instagram for a while before I got to Noma, and I knew she was the coolest, so I was very excited to meet her and work with this wonderful woman. The staff had changed during these months, and Louise was training her replacement who'd come from New York. This meant that Louise remained at Noma for only a short part of my internship, and when she left, she moved to San Francisco to work at the famous Tartine Bakery.

At Noma, in addition to our regular assignments of preparing the desserts and bread for the restaurant, we were also responsible for preparing a dessert for the staff, for the "family meal," and honestly, that was a truly fun task! The desserts we prepared at Noma were gorgeous but very precise, and were designed to relate to the food menu, so there was very little room for us pastry chefs to shine. But for the staff dessert? The sky was the limit there, and we could use our creativity to our hearts' content, and prepare anything we wanted. Louise's desserts were always stunning and always tasty, decadent, and comforting, and in the life of a chef who works 18 hours a day and rarely sits down, that's a big deal!

One day, Louise made these amazing brownies. Now I know what you're thinking: Why would a pastry chef get excited about brownies? You must have a thousand recipes for brownies! And yes, that's true, but in my opinion, brownies, like chocolate chip cookies, pound cake, and the rest of these seemingly simple dishes, still require the perfect recipe, because once you prepare it for people, they will never call it a simple dish. Between you and me, who wants dessert filled with layers, creams, and additions, when you can eat a perfect fudge brownie square?

Louise is one of the most generous and modest pastry chefs I have ever met. When I asked her for the recipe, she gave it to me immediately, and then published the recipe on her Instagram account and tagged me. Since then, it's been one of my three go-to brownie recipes that go with me everywhere.

→

→

Makes one 8-in (20-cm) square brownie pan

–

1 cup + 5 tsp (250 grams) butter

2 cups (300 grams) dark chocolate with a minimum of 60% cocoa solids, chopped

⅔ cup (100 grams) milk chocolate, chopped

2 ½ cups (500 grams) sugar

4 eggs

2 ⅓ cups (330 grams) all-purpose flour

2 ½ tsp (10 grams) baking powder

A pinch of salt

1. Preheat the oven to 170 °C (340 °F). Lightly grease a brownie baking pan and line it with parchment paper.
2. Place the chocolates and butter in a heat-proof bowl over a saucepan of simmering water (bain-marie) and heat, occasionally stirring, until melted.
3. Place the sugar and eggs in the bowl of a stand mixer fitted with the paddle attachment, and mix until pale and fluffy.
4. Reduce the speed and pour the melted chocolate mixture while mixing continuously.
5. Add the flour, baking powder, and salt, and mix until just combined (avoid overmixing).
6. Pour the batter into the baking pan and smooth the top with a spatula.
7. Bake for 30 minutes, until a toothpick inserted in the center of the pan comes out with a few moist crumbs.
8. Cool completely in the pan.

A DECADENT VERSION OF LOUISE'S AWESOME BROWNIES

During my internship at Noma, we began to see an influx of Syrian refugees arriving in Denmark. One day, Chef René Redzepi (chef and co-owner of Noma) told us that among the refugees were many children, some of whom escaped with just a single parent and sometimes without any parents at all. He thought it would a nice thing if we could make treats and hand them out to the children. However, he asked us not to talk about this "project" too much and not to discuss it on social media at all. He didn't want it to become a "big deal" or for anyone to think that we were taking a political stance on refugees, or, conversely, that this was a marketing ploy.

"They're just children," he told us. "I'm not getting into the political discussion, but I do know one thing: not too long ago, my grandparents found themselves refugees without anywhere to go. We never know what's going happen—the world is a frightening, dangerous place." René's willingness to help those in need, and to expose us to what was going on in the world at a time when we were disconnected, was, in my eyes, a blessing. I knew immediately that I was going to volunteer to help, and that I was going to go there and to meet with those children. It was important for me to see that they were all right, to understand what they were going through, to see if they needed anything, such as clothing.

So on Thursday morning, when it was my turn, I made 6 huge *gastronomes* (industrial baking trays found in professional kitchens) of Louise's brownies, but I added a few little bonus touches to make the children even happier, including:

- Reese's Peanut Butter Cups
- Crushed Twix
- Peanut butter
- Chocolate chips: bittersweet, milk, and white

It was quite a challenge to hide this abundance of decadent brownies from Noma's hungry staff, so I left them with two baking sheets and took the rest to the children. And I am so thankful and happy that I got this opportunity to bring a little bit of joy to their lives.

KING
HOME STONE K-45
MANO VINO

Section 6

Weekend Projects

#weekendvibes

Since I usually host brunches on Saturdays, I work on most weekends, so for me, weekdays and weekend projects are pretty much the same. However, for people who aren't pastry chefs and have some free time, weekends are a great opportunity to experiment with more elaborate recipes. Weekend baking lets you take on bigger challenges, and to bake recipes that take more time and patience, such as the recipes in this section. When they're done, these "projects" are truly remarkable and worth the effort.

Monkey bread is a home-baked pastry that many people associate with childhood. It is made from balls of dough rolled in butter and cinnamon-sugar, and then baked in the oven, usually in a Bundt pan. The monkey bread we know today is not the original monkey bread; the original was a loaf that was formed from pieces of leavened dough that were dipped into butter and baked, and it was popular in southern California in the 1940s. But in the middle of the twentieth century, the Hungarians and Hungarian Jews who immigrated to the United States brought with them their *arany galuska* ("golden dumpling"), or Hungarian coffee cake, in which pieces of dough were coated in cinnamon-sugar or brown sugar, and then baked. This Hungarian coffee cake then became known as monkey bread.

Once ready, the monkey bread usually disappears almost immediately—it's too delicious! Now, while I have a good recipe for monkey bread, I wanted to create something that's more unique, so I decided to put it together with pull-apart bread. Pull-apart bread is also a classic dish that's had a recent renaissance. The dough is formed into a shape with scoring so that you can pull the bread apart. The pull-apart bread is baked in loaves or squares, and it can be either savory (for example with pesto and cheese) or sweet.

So I took the monkey bread ingredients, and babka dough, and using those, I created a pull-apart bread. Since this is pull-apart bread, there are leaves instead of balls, but the flavor is of monkey bread. When the bread is ready, place the pan on the table and let everyone dig in with their hands! You can't go wrong—both monkey bread and pull-apart bread are dishes that will make you lick your fingers (this is not one of those polite pastries), and this dish is great for kids and grown-up kids (like me). This particular love child is simply irresistible!

THE LOVE CHILD OF MONKEY BREAD AND PULL-APART BREAD

Makes 2 loaf pans

-

Basic babka dough (*see recipe on page 172*)

-

For the spiced sugar

1 1/4 cup (250 grams) sugar

2 tsp cinnamon

1/2 tsp fine salt

1/2 tsp ground nutmeg

1/2 cup (110 grams) butter, melted

1 1/2 cups (150 grams) pecans, chopped

-

For the caramel glaze

1/2 cup + 1 Tbs (130 grams) brown sugar

A pinch of salt

1/4 cup (60 ml) heavy cream

1 tsp vanilla extract

1. **Prepare the spiced sugar:** Place the sugar, cinnamon, salt, and nutmeg in a bowl and mix well.

2. Grease and line two loaf pans with parchment paper.

3. Roll the dough over a lightly floured worksurface to a thickness of about 5 mm (0.2 in). Brush the dough with the melted butter and sprinkle the spiced sugar mixture and the chopped pecans.

4. Cut the dough into 3-cm (1-in) squares.

5. Make stacks of 6 squares and place the stacks vertically in the loaf pans.

6. **Prepare the caramel glaze:** Place the heavy cream and vanilla extract in a small pot and bring to a gentle simmer. Set aside.

7. Place the sugar in an even layer in a heavy-bottomed pan. Heat over a low-medium heat until the sugar begins to melt. Add a pinch of salt and cook until the sugar turns to an amber caramel.

8. **Carefully** add the warm heavy cream to the caramel while stirring continuously for about 3-5 minutes, to create a smooth, thick caramel glaze.

9. Pour the hot glaze over the cake, cover, and let rise for 30 minutes.

10. Preheat the oven to 180 °C (350 °F).

11. Bake for 35-40 minutes, until the top is a deep golden brown. Allow to rest in the pan for 20 minutes before releasing the cake from the pan and cooling on a wire rack.

Not Your Typical Restaurant Dessert

Babka or *babcia* (which means "grandmother" in Polish) is a sweet braided cake that's really popular in Israel (walk into any bakery on a Friday morning and I dare you to not find a babka there), in American Jewish cuisine, and other places that have large Jewish communities. Originally babka was baked in a babka pan, which is a Bundt-type pan shaped like an old woman's (baba's) skirt.

It's hard to forget my late Savta (grandmother) Pika's babka. She was a fantastic cook and baker, and there were a number of recipes in her repertoire that are particularly memorable. I'm pretty sure that after she passed away, my brothers wished they had one last babka from my grandmother, hidden in their freezer, you know, just in case.

Rivka (I couldn't pronounce her name so I called her Pika), my mom's mother, was born in Israel in a village called Kfar Ata that would later become Kiryat Ata, one of the northern towns in Israel. Legend has it that when my great-grandmother was pregnant with my grandmother, it was very hard to get to the local hospital in time, so my great-grandmother, who was known as "the little grandmother," was led to the hospital by my great-grandfather on a donkey. So my grandmother, the story goes, was nearly born on the back of a donkey (and you thought delivering in a car was hard!).

Both my grandmothers passed away when I was in my early twenties, before I started studying the art of pastry, so they didn't get a chance to see me become a pastry chef, or to taste my creations, at least not the ones I create as a professional pastry chef. Savta Pika would never get to see how every Friday I make dozens of babkas and sell them, or that I teach groups of people every week how to make perfect cakes, some based on her wonderful recipes. But I do wonder whether my childhood memories of my grandmother's cakes have influenced my relationship with babkas today. Is it a coincidence that babkas are an integral part of my daily baking? I'm not sure, but I do know that I'm very happy that they are, and that I can share these recipes with others.

Now, babka is not considered a restaurant dessert, so you won't find in on the menu of many chef restaurants, perhaps in none. Babka is more of a bakery dessert, something you get when you've been sitting with your bestie for a couple of hours, and decide to order a slice, thinking, at worst you and your friend won't finish it. Two hours later, only the memory of the chocolate filling and two used forks remain on the plate, and there's no sign of the babka. Babka is also an ideal dessert for a Shabbat evening meal, or a perfect Saturday morning companion to your coffee; heat up a slice just a bit and then nibble on it as you drink a huge cup of coffee during your day of rest. Chocolate babka is just perfect in every way.

I worked at several restaurants over the years where I was responsible for creating desserts. Part of my role was to come up with a new dessert menu for each season, one that combined complementary or challenging ingredients, in terms of both texture and taste. I would only bake babkas if we hosted a private event and they would ask specifically for a babka, or when I wanted to spoil the restaurant staff with a treat. When I first started hosting my own workshops, I began with a bread workshop (with minor differences, I still host that very bread workshop to this day), and in those workshops, I would teach how to make breads and chocolate babkas.
What I find most interesting is that each person likes babka somewhat differently, the same way everyone has their own take on how to make the perfect cup of instant coffee—everyone makes it for himself or herself the best, with the exact amount of coffee crystals on the spoon, and the delicate balance between milk and boiling water. A stranger will never be able to replicate that precision. The same goes for babka: There are those who love it with just a small amount of filling and a lot of dough, while others see the dough as just an excuse for the filling, which they consider the star. Then there are those who like their babka crispy, and those who prefer it so moist it's almost wet, leaving a sticky residue of syrup on their hands.

CHOCOLATE BABKA

Everyone has their take on how chocolate babka should be—and this one is mine.

Makes 1 large round babka or 2 loaves

-

For the dough

3 ¾ cups (540 grams) all-purpose flour

⅔ cup (160 ml) water

1 Tbs honey

3 Tbs (40 grams) sugar

2 eggs

3 egg yolks

2 tsp salt

2 tsp (8 grams) active dry yeast

⅓ cup (60 grams) oil

1 beaten egg, for brushing

-

For the chocolate filling

14 Tbs (200 grams) butter, at room temperature

1 cup (200 grams) sugar

1 cup (100 grams) almond flour

1 cup (100 grams) cocoa powder

2 Tbs heavy cream

A pinch of salt

1 tsp vanilla extract

1 cup chocolate chips or roughly chopped chocolate (milk/dark/white)

-

For the glaze

⅓ cup + 4 tsp (100 ml) water

1 cup (200 grams) sugar

1. **Prepare the babka dough:** Place the flour, water, honey, sugar, eggs, yolks, salt, and yeast in the bowl of a stand mixer fitted with the dough hook. Mix on a low speed until the dough comes together. Increase the speed slightly and knead for 7 minutes, until you have a soft, smooth dough.

2. Reduce to a low speed, add the oil, and knead until it's fully incorporated into the dough.

3. Shape the dough into a ball and place in a greased bowl. Cover with a towel or a loose plastic wrap and let rise for 45 minutes at room temperature.

4. Punch down the dough, cover, and let rise for another 45 minutes.

5. **Prepare the chocolate filling:** Place all of the ingredients in a bowl and mix to a smooth cream.

6. Grease and line 2 loaf pans or 1 large round cake pan with parchment paper.

7. Place the dough on a lightly floured worksurface and roll into an 80×25-cm (10×32-in) rectangle, about 3-5 mm (0.1-0.2 in) thick.

8. Spread an even layer of the chocolate filling all the way to the edges. Starting with the long side, roll into a tight coil. Slice the coil in half, into 2 coils.

9. Slice the coil in half lengthwise, to expose the filling. Twist the halves together like a screw. Place each babka in a loaf pan, or arrange both babkas inside the round cake pan.

10. Brush with a thin coat of the beaten egg and let rise uncovered for 30–40 minutes at room temperature.

11. Preheat the oven to 180 °C (350 °F).

12. Brush the babka with the beaten egg a second time, and bake for 25–35 minutes, until dark brown and baked through.

13. **Prepare the glaze:** Place the sugar and water in a saucepan and bring to a boil. Set aside.

14. Brush the babka with the hot syrup as soon as it comes out of the oven. This will give it a shiny glaze and lock the moisture in.

15. Cool to room temperature before releasing from the pan.

CHOCOLATE HAZELNUT *KRANTZ* CAKE

When I first started to make my cakes, I used to make Krantz cake with a classic chocolate filling that's very much like my rugelach filling—not super sweet but very rich and full of butter and cocoa. My customers loved the cake and used to wait in line to buy it, and then one day I asked one of them what he wanted to buy and he said "babka with Nutella®." I was not surprised; I myself love hazelnut cream, and the people who love babka fall into two categories: those who love the version that's a bit more rich and bitter, and those who need the sweetness of the nuts and chocolate combined.

Nowadays I always make both, so I make sure to give them each a unique look to be able to differentiate them. My chocolate cake is braided, whereas the hazelnut Krantz is shaped like a rose. I love them both. I add Gianduja chocolate to the Krantz, and it is a very important part of the recipe. Just remember that in this cake, the important part is the dough rather than the filling, which is simply ready-made hazelnut cream.

Makes 1 Bundt pan

–

Basic babka dough (*see recipe on page 172*)

1 beaten egg, for brushing

–

For the filling

1½ jars (19.5 oz or 525 grams) chocolate hazelnut spread

2 cups (350 grams) Gianduja or milk chocolate, chopped

–

For the glaze

½ cup (100 grams) sugar

¼ cup + 2 tsp (70 ml) water

1. Grease a Bundt cake pan.

2. Place the babka dough on a lightly floured worksurface and roll into a 20×50-cm (8×20-in) rectangle, 5 mm (0.2 in) thick.

3. Spread an even layer of the chocolate hazelnut spread all the way to the edges. Sprinkle the chopped chocolate on top.

4. Starting with the long side, roll the rectangle into a tight coil. Cut the coil into 2 equal coils, and then cut each coil into 5 equal pieces, for a total of 10 pieces. Place in the baking tray, cut side facing up.

5. Brush the dough with a thin layer of the beaten egg (and if you can, try to avoid brushing the chocolate filling) and let rise uncovered for 1 hour at room temperature.

6. Preheat the oven to 180 °C (350 °F).

7. Bake for 45 minutes, until dark brown and baked through.

8. While the Krantz cake is baking, **prepare the glaze:** Place the sugar and the water in a saucepan and bring to a boil. Set aside.

9. Brush the cake with the hot syrup as soon as it comes out of the oven. This will give it a shiny glaze and lock the moisture in. Let cool to room temperature before releasing from the pan.

SAVORY BABKA WITH CHEESES, PESTO, AND ROASTED VEGETABLES

This was a savory babka I created for Shavuot one year; it's gone through several iterations. At first, since it seemed like a cool idea, I just took brioche dough and filled it with cheese and roasted vegetables. Then I just rolled the dough and the other ingredients and made a braided cake—and the result was super successful.

At some point I started to use the dough I make for babka—and that was an even bigger hit. When I make my savory babkas for Shavuot they're very much in demand and always sell out.

Makes 2 babka loaves

–

For the dough

4 cups minus 1 Tbs (550 grams) all-purpose flour

2/3 cup (160 ml) water

2 tsp (8 grams) active dry yeast

1/2 cup (100 grams) sugar

2 tsp salt

2 eggs

2 egg yolks

1/4 cup (60 ml) olive oil

–

For the filling

3.5 oz (100 grams) pesto

1 cup (100 grams) Parmesan cheese, grated

14 oz (400 grams) chèvre goat cheese, cut into 5-mm (0.2-in) slices

4 cups of your choice of roasted vegetables (peppers/ hot chili peppers/ eggplant/ zucchini/ broccoli...)

–

For the topping

1 beaten egg, for brushing

1 tsp aromatic herbs such as rosemary or thyme

1. **Prepare the dough:** Place the flour, water, yeast, sugar, salt, eggs, and yolks in the bowl of a stand mixer fitted with the dough hook. Mix on a low speed until the dough comes together. Increase the speed and knead for 7-10 minutes, until you have a soft, smooth dough.

2. Reduce to a low speed, add the oil, and knead until it's fully incorporated into the dough; this step may take several minutes, so be patient.

3. Shape the dough into a ball and place in a greased bowl. Cover with a towel or a loose plastic wrap and let rise for 1 1/2 hours at room temperature, until it doubles in volume.

4. Punch down the dough, cover, and let rise for another 45 minutes.

5. Grease and line 2 loaf pans with parchment paper.

6. Place the dough on a lightly floured worksurface and divide into 2 equal pieces. Roll each piece into a 20×30-cm (8×12-in) rectangle, 5 mm (0.2 in) thick.

7. Spread each rectangle with an even layer of pesto all the way to the edges. Sprinkle the grated Parmesan and scatter the roasted vegetables. Place the rounds of chèvre goat cheese between the vegetables.

8. Starting with the long side, roll each rectangle into a tight coil, tucking in any bits that slide out.

9. Slice each coil in half and twist the halves together like a screw. Place each "screw" in a loaf pan.

10. Brush the babka with the beaten egg, and let rise uncovered for 40–60 minutes at room temperature.

11. Preheat the oven to 180 °C (350 °F).

12. Brush the babka with the beaten egg and sprinkle the aromatic herbs.

13. Bake for 25–35 minutes.

14. Cool in the pan for 10 minutes.

15. Serve warm or at room temperature.

Section 7

Special Occasions

Some recipes remind me of a specific moment: like the time my mom and I rode the train from Tokyo to Osaka, and ate an entire cheesecake; or my niece's birthday, when she asked me to make a s'mores cake. To me, a recipe or a pastry isn't just about that bite—it's about everything that's wrapped in the memory of that moment, which takes me back in time. This chapter is dedicated to those memories, to keep them alive so that they aren't just frozen in time.

I grew up in an Eastern European family of Ashkenazi Jews: On my father's side the family hailed from Bulgaria, and on my mom's side, my grandfather came from Vienna, Austria, and my grandmother came from an Israeli family going back several generations (although originally, they were from some combination of Poland, Russia, or Ukraine). I was lucky to have all four of my grandparents growing up (which is more than many children can say); however, my family was quite small, so that even my extended family included fewer than 10 people. In fact, my brother is the eldest grandchild, while I'm the youngest one.

Because I was the youngest grandchild, my grandparents were all quite elderly, so I don't have any memories of cooking or baking with them. By the time I was 24, both of my grandmothers (Rivka and Victoria) had passed away, which is why I don't have any experience of cooking or baking with them in the kitchen. My mom and I often commiserate about how so many of her mom's recipes have been lost, which is truly a pity, and we talk about trying to recreate those amazing recipes. That sense of missing out, of learning from that generation, is something I keep trying to overcome in my kitchen. Someday I plan to go to my mom and ask for her recipes and then begin to make everything with butter instead of margarine; now that will be a true joy for me, so get ready! Sometimes I ask myself what my grandmothers would have said about my career choice. Would they have been happy about the way in which food has become a way of life and of showing love? I think so, since it was their way too.

I also feel that it's up to me to correct the misperception held by many in Israel that Ashkenazi Jewish food is bland and lacking any flavor. Since I'm half Bulgarian and half Austrian-Polish (and also very Israeli)—that misperception really bothers me! I know for a fact that there are wonderful, mouthwatering dishes that my grandmothers used to make and my mom makes to this day, and this is a chance to show everyone just how truly great that food can be.

Family as Inspiration

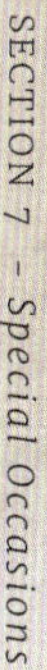

MARBLE CAKE

As a child I remember that when my mom went into the kitchen to cook or bake, she had this box of index cards with the recipes written on them. She also had a lot of paper cuttings from newspapers with recipes she liked and saved in that box. Some of the recipes were written during the austerity period in Israel in the 1950s, when butter was scarce, so the recipes used margarine instead: Blueband Margarine (vegetable oil) and Goldband Margarine (which contains some dairy). These recipes were her mother's recipes, and among them was a marble cake, a cake that was served at every occasion I can remember. Savta Rivka (whom I called Savta Pika) used to make that marble cake, and then my mom made it, and then I made it with my mom. But the first time I actually felt this recipe was being handed down from generation to generation was when I lived in New York, and I wanted to bake a cake for the weekend. I asked my mom to send me the recipe, and after I made the cake, I felt like I was home.

When I returned to Israel, I made the marble cake again using loaf pans. When my mom saw the cakes, she said the cakes were so precise, they looked store-bought, and I was so pleased. The great thing about this cake is that it isn't plain; it doesn't require any butter—only oil and milk—but it's perfect for all occasions.

Makes 2 loaf pans or 1 Bundt cake pan

For the cake

- 6 eggs
- A pinch of salt
- 1 tsp vanilla extract
- 1 3/4 cups (350 grams) sugar
- 1 cup (240 ml) whole milk
- 1 cup (210 grams) extra virgin olive oil
- 2 1/2 cups (350 grams) self-rising flour
- 2 Tbs cocoa powder

For the glaze

- 3 Tbs (40 grams) butter
- 1/2 cup (80 grams) dark chocolate, chopped

1. Preheat the oven to 170 °C (340 °F) and butter 2 loaf cake pans or a Bundt cake pan.

2. Place the eggs, salt, and sugar in the bowl of a stand mixer fitted with the whisk attachment, and beat to an airy, yet stiff cream. Add the vanilla extract.

3. Place the milk and olive oil in a bowl. Reduce the mixer speed to low and pour in a quarter of the liquid mixture followed by a third of the flour. Repeat this with the remaining liquids and flour, alternating between them and ending with the liquid. Mix until the batter is smooth with no lumps, but don't overmix.

→

→

4. Divide the batter equally between 2 bowls. Add the cocoa to one bowl and mix until fully incorporated.

5. Divide the vanilla mixture between the cake pans and pour the chocolate mixture on top. Use a sharp knife or a metal skewer to swirl the chocolate mixture through the vanilla to create a marble effect.

6. Bake for 30–40 minutes, until a skewer inserted in the center of the cake comes out clean with a few moist crumbs. Cool to room temperature.

7. **Prepare the glaze:** Place the chocolate and butter in a heat-proof bowl over a saucepan of simmering water (bain-marie) and stir to a smooth cream. Remove from the heat and let cool for several minutes.

8. Transfer the cake to a serving plate and pour the glaze over the cake.

CHEESE AND ZA'ATAR (HYSSOP) PESTO PRETZELS

My mom and I share a love of theatre and musicals, so whenever we go overseas, we always see a good show, whether in New York or in London. After the show, we're always starving, so we go to look for something that's open late and still has a decent offering. In New York, this was often a hot, fresh pretzel with cheese or even plain.

A few years ago I was in Long Island, hosting a workshop on baking, at the home of this really lovely woman, who made an amazing pesto from za'atar (hyssop) that she'd "smuggled" from Israel (so we're not going to give her name away!). When I tasted the pesto I thought "Wow, what a wonderful idea to make pesto from za'atar! How come I didn't think of that myself?" The flavor was wonderful and very concentrated and perfect. After that, the idea of hyssop pesto stuck with me, so every season I would buy hyssop and make the pesto. Nowadays I have my own window planter with hyssop that lets me make it year-round.

I also think that in the last year, fresh hyssop has come into its own, and that more people are using it in their cooking. It used to be that people would only buy dried hyssop at the spice shop, but now they're buying the fresh leaves at the market and using those. And I am too: I love the idea of using fresh hyssop in my baking and cooking, and I've used it in a few pastries, such as crème brulee, or mixed it with fried onion on pitas or on bialy. It's a truly wonderful herb that has a very strong flavor, which gave me the idea of mixing this very Middle Eastern herb with a very European pastry, pretzels.

Now, it's not always possible to find the herb fresh, but then I wrote that I was looking for fresh hyssop in one of my blog posts, and one of my followers, who came to a workshop, brought me this huge bag full of fresh hyssop and said, "I saw that you were looking for this so I brought it to you." And I was so happy, and so moved, and I knew that with this amount of hyssop I had to make pesto. So I put Uri, my significant other, to the task of removing each leaf from its stem, but I didn't tell him what I was going to do with them (he probably thought I was nuts, why would I need so much hyssop?). Then I made the hyssop pesto and I let him try it and he said, "Hyssop pesto?" and I answered, "Yes, yes, try it." So he did. And he then he said, "Holy s**t this is amazing" and he was ready to take the entire glass jar of pesto and eat it there and then, without any bread (well, maybe with some bread). Then, as we were preparing for a shoot for this book, I prepared another jar of pesto, and when he saw it he started "wagging his tail" and asking for it, so I made us a tomato and mozzarella salad and put the pesto on top and he loved it. Even though he's not a huge fan of mozzarella.

And that's what gave me the idea of creating a cheese and za'atar (hyssop)-pesto pretzel.

Makes 6 pretzels

-

For the pretzel dough

2 1/2 cups (360 grams) bread flour

2 Tbs (15 grams) fresh yeast (or 1 tsp (5 grams) active dry yeast)

3/4 cup + 1 Tbs (200ml) water

1 1/2 Tbs (20 grams) extra virgin olive oil

1 tsp salt

3 Tbs butter, melted

A handful of mozzarella cheese, grated

A handful of Parmesan cheese, grated

-

For the filling and topping

Za'atar (hyssop) pesto (*see recipe below*)

3 Tbs butter, melted

1/2 cup mozzarella cheese, grated

1/2 cup Parmesan cheese, grated

-

For the za'atar (hyssop) pesto

A bunch of fresh za'atar (hyssop) leaves or any other green herb you prefer

2/3 cup (100 grams) cashew nuts

2–3 Tbs grated Parmesan cheese

1/2 tsp salt

About 1/2 cup extra virgin olive oil

1. **Prepare the pesto:** Separate the leaves and place in the bowl of a food processor. Add the cashew nuts, Parmesan cheese, and 2 tablespoons of olive oil and blend to a coarse paste.

2. Scrape the sides of the bowl, add the salt, and blend to a smoother consistency. Taste and add more salt if needed.

3. If the pesto is too thick, drizzle more olive oil while blending to reach your preferred consistency. Refrigerate until ready to use.

4. **Prepare the dough:** Place the flour, yeast, water, oil, and salt in the bowl of a stand mixer fitted with the dough hook and mix on a low speed for 2 minutes, until the dough comes together. Increase to a medium speed and knead for 15 minutes. The dough should be smooth and not stick to the sides of the bowl.

5. Place the dough on a lightly floured worksurface, divide into 6 equal parts, and roll into logs. Cover with a towel and let rest for 10 minutes.

6. Line a tray with parchment paper.

7. Roll each dough log into a 30×5-cm (12×2-in) rectangle and spread an even layer of the pesto, leaving the edges clean. Evenly sprinkle some of the grated cheeses on top. Brush the edges lightly with water, roll tightly into a coil, and twist into a pretzel shape. Lightly press to seal the edges and transfer to the baking tray.

8. Cover and let rise for 30 minutes.

9. Preheat the oven to 245 °C (475 °F).

10. Brush the pretzels with the melted butter and sprinkle the grated cheese on top.

11. Bake for 10–15 minutes, until the pretzels are golden brown.

Marzipan/Masapan to Make My Grandma Proud

I am half Bulgarian, on my father's side. And in Bulgarian families, home-made marzipan (a Bulgarian treat) is a part of every occasion: When it's time to celebrate or to mourn, marzipan is always there.

I'm sorry to say that I was not particularly close to my grandmothers; I've often heard stories about people who learned to cook by working with their grandmothers in the kitchen, but that was not my experience. Instead, I learned to cook with my mom, my pillar of fire, the woman who let me hold a wooden spoon for the first time, the woman who let me help her prepare cakes at night before I was even 10 using a hand mixer, in our Ra'anana kitchen where I grew up. I was the youngest child and the youngest grandchild in my family, so I treated my rather elderly grandparents with respect and awe; I didn't really know how to approach them, and by the time I was old enough to understand that there was so much I could learn from them, they were already gone.

I found my path into my grandmothers' kitchen on my own, using my hands, through the stories, the traditions, and through their old recipe boxes. My mom had learned how to cook through my grandmothers, both her mother and mother-in-law, which I find admirable, and even today she has many of their old recipes, although others have been lost and we can only try to recreate them.

I made my first marzipan while working at Raphael (one of the best restaurants in Tel Aviv, although it's closed since). We used to make marzipan once or twice a week, either almond or pistachio, and it would be used in Raphael's famous petit fours plate, which was served as a dessert. The marzipan I made there was the first marzipan I liked in a long time, because it was really, really good. Until then, marzipan for me was something you could buy in the supermarket, usually covered with chocolate, which looked wonderful, but then, after you tasted it, was truly awful. I came to realize that the marzipan we made at Raphael was very similar to the masapan my Bulgarian grandmother used to make. The Bulgarians don't call it marzipan, but *masapan*, and they make it from whole almonds, which they soak in water until the skin detaches from the almond on its own. Then, the almond is ground and mixed with syrup until the texture is perfect, almost like playdough, and the you can mold it into different shapes.

The next time I made marzipan was while I was studying in New York, during my confectionary studies unit. This marzipan was just as good, but very different; it was harder, thicker, and a lot less cookie-like than masapan. Toward the end of my pastry studies we had a final test, and one of the tests was to create a wedding cake from scratch. An entire wedding cake, inspired by a wedding book that had been prepared by the following year's class, who would also choose the winning cake among those we created.

Anyway, during my studies, my culinary professors discovered I had a talent for decorating cakes. I had no idea I had this talent, because cake decoration wasn't something I had a chance to do while I was in Israel. Cake decoration is a very niche field of baking, and I would later have the opportunity to apply this ability while studying in the United States, and then again while interning with the celebrity chef Ron Ben-Israel, at his wedding cake design studio (RBI Cakes) in New York. I was very excited at the prospect of the wedding cake project, and, while my classmates all decorated their cakes with fondant icing, I decorated an entire cake with fondipan, which is a combination of fondant and marzipan. Fondipan has the elasticity of both the fondant and marzipan, but also has marzipan's unique coloring, which I think adds a lovely beige that's perfect for a wedding cake, even more than the traditional (old-fashioned) white. Fondipan is also tastier and has a more complex flavor than sugar (which is the flavor of fondant), because it contains a nuttiness and the real taste of almonds. So it's both prettier and better tasting, making it the best of all worlds.

I'm sorry to say that my cake didn't win (and I don't even have pictures of it, since this was before the advent of smartphones with their advanced cameras). But I'm still very proud of it and of the way it turned out even today. The class of the following year chose a different cake. After they made their selection, my chef instructor during that period, Chef Tom Jones (a former Marine), who was one of the toughest chefs I encountered during my studies, came up to me and said, "I will never understand the choices made by the classes in these competitions, but know this: your cake should have won." Now, I'm a pretty competitive person, so I can't claim that his words didn't matter because I was very proud of my cake. In fact, they mattered a lot. His warm words moved me and made me feel a million times better because they came from a chef who was no pushover. I knew that choosing marzipan, because of its flavor and, in many ways, because of my heritage, was the right choice.

Marzipan (or masapan) is one of the confections that Bulgarians serve on all happy occasions. It's always served on a big, lavish tray, symbolizing wealth and sweetness, complex like life. Because it's parve and gluten-free, it's perfect for everyone. So here are my recipes for marzipan that's worth making.

ALMOND OR PISTACHIO MARZIPAN/MASAPAN

Makes 80 pieces

-

For almond marzipan

1 cup (250 ml) (orgeat) almond syrup, available online and in specialty stores

1 cup (200 grams) sugar

½ lemon, juiced

3 ½ cups (500 grams) peeled almonds, ground

A few drops of rosewater (optional)

-

For pistachio marzipan

10 Tbs (150 ml) (orgeat) almond syrup, available online and in specialty stores

½ cup (100 grams) sugar

½ lemon, juiced

1 ¼ cups (175 grams) ground shelled pistachios

1 oz (25 grams) pistachio paste, available online and in specialty stores

-

For the sugar crust

2 cups (400 grams) sugar

1. Place the almond syrup, sugar, and lemon juice in a wide pot over medium heat and bring to a gentle boil, stirring occasionally.

2. Grind the almonds/pistachios a second time. Place them in the bowl of a stand mixer fitted with the paddle attachment.

3. Pour the boiling almond syrup into the mixer while mixing on a high speed until you end up with a smooth, pliable dough. Add the rosewater, if using. Transfer to a bowl, cover, and refrigerate for 30 minutes.

4. Divide into 3 equal parts and roll each piece into a rope 1 cm (0.4 in) in diameter. Sprinkle sugar on the worksurface and roll the marzipan ropes in the sugar so they are fully coated. Using a knife, cut into 2-cm (0.8-in) pieces.

5. Roll each piece in the sugar, and then squeeze lightly in the middle into small "gnocchi" shapes.

6. Transfer to a serving plate.

SIGAL'S COFFEE CAKE

My sister-in-law Sigal has a favorite Bundt coffee cake with a nut streusel in the middle. After my brother met Sigal, my rich coffee cake became her signature favorite cake, requested for every occasion. When they met, my brother had just opened a bar in Tel Aviv. All the "movers and shakers" attended his grand opening because Sigal is in the TV business. At the time, I was doing my military service, so I also came to the opening and brought a coffee cake that I used to make a lot then (I'd been making it since I was in middle school). Everyone tried the cake and loved it, including Sigal and her friends.

Since then, Sigal has claimed this cake as her own, and she always asks for it, so it's become known as Sigal's Coffee Cake. But there's a bit of a catch there: Sometimes I make the cake when Sigal is on a detox and can't eat it; and sometimes I don't make the cake, and she's disappointed since she can finally eat her favorite cake. And then, once in a blue moon, everything aligns properly, and the timing is right for me to make and bring the cake, and for her to eat it too!

→

Makes 1 Bundt cake pan

-

For the cake

14 Tbs (200 grams) butter at room temperature

1 1/2 cups (150 grams) powdered sugar

3 eggs

1 shot of double espresso

1 1/2 tsp vanilla extract

1 1/4 cups (250 grams) sour cream

2 1/2 cups (350 grams) all-purpose flour

1/2 tsp baking soda

2 1/2 tsp (10 grams) baking powder

1/2 tsp salt

-

For the streusel

1/4 cup (50 grams) light brown cane sugar

1/2 cup (70 grams) all-purpose flour

1 1/2 tsp cinnamon

1/4 tsp salt

3 1/2 Tbs (50 grams) butter at room temperature

3/4 cup (90 grams) walnuts

-

For the glaze

1 cup (100 grams) powdered sugar

4-6 Tbs maple syrup

1. Preheat the oven to 180 °C (350 °F) and grease a Bundt cake pan generously.

2. Place the butter and powdered sugar in the bowl of a stand mixer fitted with the paddle attachment, and mix until pale and fluffy.

3. Add the eggs one after the other, beating well after each addition. Add the espresso shot, vanilla extract, and sour cream and mix well.

4. Add the flour, baking soda, baking powder, and salt, and mix until just combined (avoid overmixing). Set aside.

5. **Prepare the streusel:** Place all of the ingredients in a bowl and mix with your hand until you create a crumbly mixture resembling coarse sand.

6. Pour 1/3 of the cake batter into the cake pan and sprinkle half of the streusel on top, making sure to spread it evenly. Pour another 1/3 of the cake batter on top and sprinkle the remaining streusel on top. Pour the remaining cake batter and smooth to an even layer.

7. Bake 45-50 minutes, until golden. The cake is ready when a toothpick inserted in the center comes out clean. Cool the cake in the pan before turning it over on a serving plate.

8. **Prepare the glaze:** Place the powdered sugar, and maple syrup in a bowl and mix well. Drizzle over the cake.

A Tale of Three Mixers

For years my mom had a simple stand mixer that worked "like a boss," but she dreamed of getting a KitchenAid™ mixer, a dream that would later become my dream. I think it was when I was in high school that she finally bought her KitchenAid, the same one she still uses to this day. It was shiny and black, and she was so happy with it, probably as happy as I was a few years later, when I bought my first mixer. At the time, I was a student, living in New York, in a small studio apartment in Harlem. My pastry studies took place in Soho, so I was commuting to Soho every morning, and I used to come home every day with at least two cakes we'd baked in class that day.

At first, I didn't think I needed a mixer; my older brother, Amit, was also living in New York at that time, together with my sister-in-law and my niece, and on some weekends, I'd come by and share the wealth. But—I did say at least two cakes every day—right? So at a certain point they said: "Look, we love you, but stop bringing cakes!" It wasn't until my niece's birthday, when she asked for a princess cake, that I realized I didn't have a mixer! How was I supposed to make her anything but brownies without a mixer? At which point my other brother, Yoav, who's a musician living in Australia (so not quite on our block), said: "You not owning a mixer is like me not owning a piano." Point taken.

Yoav wired me the money that day and sent me off to buy my very first KitchenAid (which I still have to this day, although I've acquired two more since). It was red, or to be specific, "cinnamon glow," and it was bigger than the one my mom had. My mixer had a handle for lifting the bowl up, and I remember that joyful taxi ride home from Bed, Bath & Beyond on the Upper West Side, carefully holding my shiny, new mixer on my knees.

S'MORES LAYER CAKE WITH SPECULOOS CREAM AND SCORCHED MERINGUE FROSTING

When I became a pastry chef, I came up with my own super special birthday cake: a decadent s'mores layer cake that's as sinful as it sounds.

Makes one 20–22-cm (8–8½-in) springform pan

–

For the chocolate cake

1 cup + 5 tsp (250 grams) butter, cut into cubes

1 ⅔ cups (250 grams) dark chocolate with a minimum of 60% cocoa solids, chopped

2 Tbs instant coffee granules

¾ cup (180 ml) boiling water

¾ cup (90 grams) self-rising flour

1 cup (140 grams) all-purpose flour

½ tsp baking soda

½ cup (70 grams) cocoa powder

1 ¾ cup (350 grams) sugar

4 eggs

2 Tbs extra virgin olive oil

½ cup (120 ml) buttermilk

–

For the speculoos cream

4 cups + 2 Tbs (950 grams) heavy whipping cream

1 jar (400 grams) smooth speculoos spread

1.7 oz (50 grams) milk chocolate

A pinch of salt

–

For the meringue frosting

5 egg whites (150 grams)

¾ cup + 3 Tbs (185 grams) sugar

A pinch of salt

1. **The day before, prepare the speculoos cream:** Place the heavy cream and salt in a pot and bring to a gentle simmer.

2. Place the speculoos spread and the milk chocolate in a bowl. Pour the simmering cream, and let stand for 1 minute before mixing to a smooth cream. Transfer to an airtight container and cool to room temperature before placing in the refrigerator overnight.

3. **Prepare the cake:** Preheat the oven to 160 °C (320 °F). Grease and line a springform pan with parchment paper.

4. Place the butter, chocolate, coffee granules, and water in a pot and cook over a low heat until smooth, stirring occasionally.

5. Place the flours, baking soda, cocoa, and sugar in a bowl and mix well.

→

6. Place the eggs, olive oil, and buttermilk in a separate bowl and beat well.

7. Add the flour mixture to the egg mixture and mix until just combined (avoid overmixing). Add the melted chocolate mixture and mix to a smooth batter without lumps. Pour the batter into the cake pan and smooth with a spatula.

8. Bake for 1 ½–2 hours. The cake is ready when a toothpick inserted in the center comes out clean. Cool to room temperature.

9. **Assemble the cake:** Slice the cake horizontally into 3 equal slices. Place the bottom slice on a serving plate and spread an even layer of the spéculoos cream. Place the middle cake slice on top and spread an even layer of the spéculoos cream. Cover with the top cake slice and frost the top and sides of the cake with the remaining speculoos cream. Refrigerate the cake while preparing the meringue.

10. **Prepare the meringue:** Place the egg whites, sugar, and salt in a heat-proof bowl over a saucepan of simmering water (bain-marie) and beat until the sugar has completely dissolved.

11. Transfer to the bowl of a stand mixer fitted with the whip attachment and beat into stiff peaks.

12. Frost the cake with the meringue. Using a kitchen torch, toast the meringue until nicely browned.

When I was a child, my mom would make an icebox (frozen) cake for every birthday, and only on birthdays. The cake is made up of three layers: The bottom layer is made of crushed meringue kisses; the second layer is a thick chocolate mousse; and the top layer is whipped cream. The cake is placed in the freezer overnight, and then, on the following day, we all engage in the process of "straightening" the cake until it's gone!

My childhood birthdays were always a celebration (in fact even today my birthdays are a celebration). My mom would always wake me up with a cake with candles, in bed, so that going to sleep the night before I was always excited and full of anticipation for the coming day. I would wake up and put out the candles, and because the cake was always an ice cream cake, we'd have to put it back in the freezer immediately. I would start the day with a slice of birthday cake, and my mom, who always invested a lot of thought and effort in our birthdays, would have a scavenger hunt for my gifts, which she hid throughout the house (she would hide a lot of little gifts). Then we'd spend the day doing something that I liked, such as going to a jewelry factory. When I became a teenager I preferred to have my friends come over and spend time with me, but now that I think about it, having a day out with my mom was so much better. What was I thinking?

Nowadays, because I'm a pastry chef, everyone is afraid to make me a birthday cake because they're afraid it won't be up to standard. So no one makes me a cake anymore, and that's very sad.

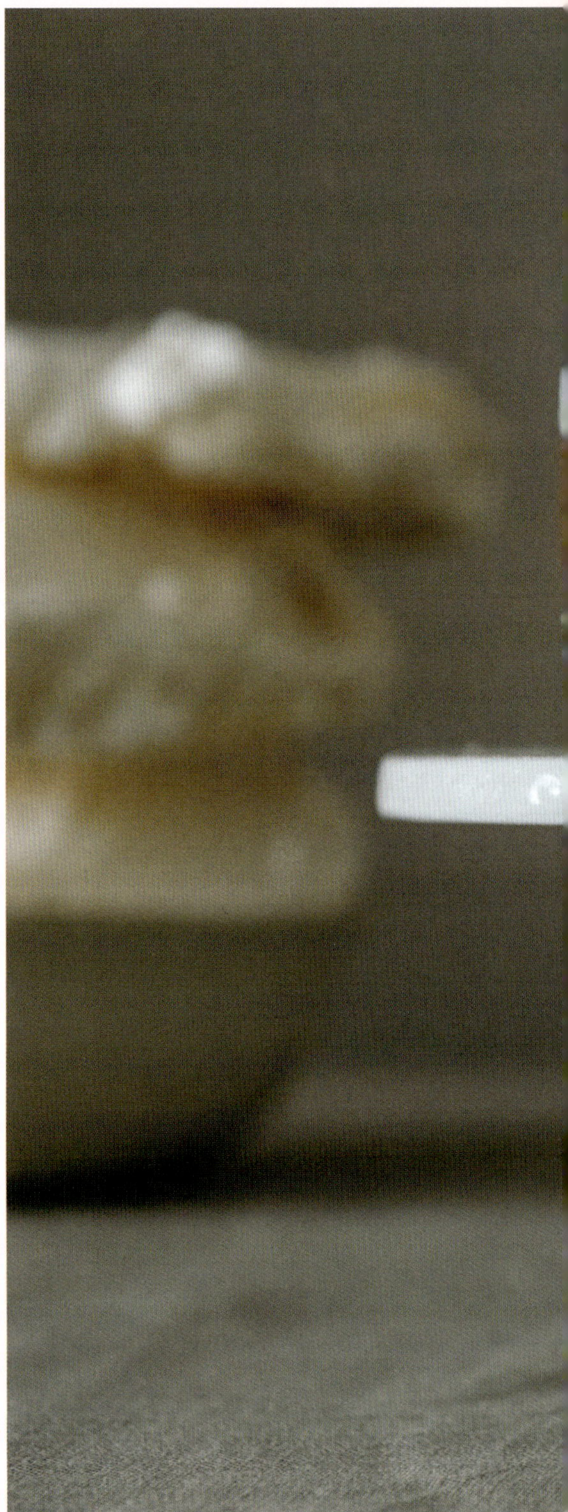

MY MOM'S ICEBOX BIRTHDAY CAKE: IT'S NOT A BIRTHDAY WITHOUT BIRTHDAY CAKE

Makes one 24-26-cm (9-10-in) springform pan

-

For the meringue base*

6–7 (250 grams) egg whites

A pinch of salt

1 ½ cups (300 grams) sugar

*Alternatively, use 2–3 giant meringues or 10-12 standard-sized store-bought meringue kisses, crushed

-

For the chocolate mousse

1 cup (150 grams) dark chocolate with a minimum of 60% cocoa solids, chopped

½ cup (100 grams) butter

1 tsp instant coffee granules

3 eggs, separated

½ cup (100 grams) sugar

1 Tbs cognac (optional)

½ cup (50 grams) ground hazelnuts (optional)

A pinch of salt

-

For the whipped cream

1 cup (250 ml) heavy cream

3 Tbs powdered sugar

1. **Prepare the meringue:** Place the egg whites and salt in the bowl of a stand mixer fitted with the whip attachment and beat at medium speed for several minutes until soft peaks form.

2. Add 1–2 tablespoons of sugar, and beat for 1–2 minutes. Repeat this, adding 1–2 tablespoons and beating well until all of the sugar dissolves.

3. Increase to a high speed and beat until stiff peaks form.

4. Preheat the oven to 90 °C (200 °F) and line a baking tray with parchment paper.

5. Transfer the meringue to a piping bag and pipe kisses, evenly spaced, on the parchment paper. Alternatively, spoon the meringue on the baking tray freestyle.

6. Bake for 10 hours, until the meringue is baked through. Cool.

7. Place the meringue in a zip locked bag and crush gently with a rolling pin to large chunks. Place at the bottom of the cake pan in an even layer.

8. **Prepare the chocolate mousse:** Place the chocolate and butter in a heat-proof bowl over a saucepan of simmering water (bain-marie) and heat, stirring occasionally, until melted. Add the instant coffee granules, mix, and set aside.

9. Place the egg yolks, ¼ cup of sugar, and the cognac (if using) in the bowl of a stand mixer fitted with the paddle attachment, and mix until pale and fluffy.

→

10. Reduce the speed and pour the melted chocolate mixture while mixing continuously. Gently fold in the ground hazelnuts (if using).

11. Place the egg whites and salt in the clean bowl of a stand mixer fitted with the whip attachment and beat at medium speed for several minutes until soft peaks form.

12. Add the remaining 1/4 cup of sugar, and beat until stiff peaks form.

13. Gently fold 1/3 of the whipped egg whites into the chocolate mixture. Add the remaining whipped egg whites and gently fold.

14. Pour the chocolate mousse over the crushed meringues, cover, and place in the freezer for 1–2 hours.

15. **Prepare the whipped cream:** Whip the cream and powdered sugar to soft peaks. Pour over the chocolate mousse and smooth to an even layer. Cover and freeze overnight.

16. Serve frozen.

There are certain moments in life that demand a recipe that's truly unique and special. Often, they're connected to a specific person or a memory, but they remain with us, and for me, the following recipes are each linked to a unique, unforgettable moment.

Unforgettable Moments

When Mom and I Finished an Entire Cheesecake in Japan

The second time I went to Japan was with my mom; it was a very special trip, and we planned it around the time of the cherry blossom (Sakura). The trip I planned revolved mostly around food (of course), and Japanese culture and cuisine. I really wanted my mom to feel the true Japanese experience of street food and the Japanese interpretation of French food. Of course, there are many noteworthy and unique pastries that originate from Japan, but the French pastries there are excellent (in Japan they do just about everything well). You'll find every French pastry there in perfect form, and French chefs who've opened their own places there because the locals are obsessed with French pastry.

The best way to travel between cities in Japan is via the Shinkansen train (the bullet train). The train stations there are an experience in and of themselves. Everything is so clean.

After we made our way out of the train station in Osaka, we decided to grab a taxi to the hotel, but then we saw a store that sold cheesecakes that looked really cool (to be honest, I'm not sure we realized that it was a cheesecake store at first). We decided to buy a whole cake—20 centimeters in diameter—and they asked us if we planned to eat it soon or not (meaning did we plan to take it on the train). We said we did, so they gave us the cake inside a neat little cooler. As it turns out, had we said we were not going to eat it immediately they would not have sold it to us because this cake simply doesn't keep.

Next, we bought a couple of bento boxes for lunch and took everything to our hotel room. After we ate the bento, we tried the cheesecake, which was covered with apricot jelly, and then it hit us—the incredible flavor of the cake. Now, because we'd just had a full lunch, initially we each took a small piece, optimistic that it would be enough. It was like nothing I'd ever eaten before. The taste of brie inside the cheesecake was phenomenal, a truly out-of-body experience. In case I forgot to mention, this was a BRIE cheesecake!!! Before we knew it, we'd finished an entire cake! My mom and I remember that experience and remind each other about it constantly, and you know what, if I had the chance, I would go back to Osaka just to have that cake again.

Had there been an option of bringing the cake to Israel I'm sure we would have bought another one, but as the store emphasized, the cake didn't travel well. I'm actually very pleased that not everyone knows about this cake because it's our secret from Japan.

BRIE CHEESECAKE

Makes one 20-cm (8-in) springform pan

–

For the base

1 1/2–2 cups ground graham crackers, speculoos, or petit beurre shortbread cookies

3 Tbs (40 grams) cold butter

–

For the cheesecake

3/4 cup (150 grams) sugar

7 oz (200 grams) cream cheese

16.5 oz (470 grams) Brie cheese, blended in a food processor until smooth

4 eggs

1/2 cup (120 grams) heavy cream

1 1/2 tsp vanilla extract

1/2 tsp salt

–

For the glaze

About 1 1/2 cups (350 grams) apricot jam

2–3 Tbs water

1. **The day before:** Grease and line a springform pan with parchment paper.

2. Place the crackers or cookies and the butter in the bowl of a food processor and blend to a mixture resembling wet sand.

3. Transfer the mixture to the pan and press evenly to the base. Freeze for 20 minutes.

4. **Prepare the cheesecake filling:** Place a roasting pan filled with water at the bottom of the oven to create a humid environment, and preheat the oven to 150 °C (300 °F).

5. Place the sugar, cream cheese, Brie, eggs, heavy cream, vanilla extract, and salt in a food processor and blend to a smooth soft cream.

6. Pour the batter over the frozen crust and bake for 30 minutes until the cake is just set. Turn off the oven, open the oven door slightly and let the cake sit until the oven has cooled. Cool the cake to room temperature before covering with plastic wrap and refrigerating overnight.

7. **The next day:** Release the cake from the pan and place on a serving plate.

8. Place the apricot jam and the water in a small pot and bring to a boil.

9. Glaze the cake. Cool.

Brooklyn-Tokyo Bound

A few years ago I went with a friend on a bakery tour in Brooklyn, around the time when Brooklyn was starting to become an "it" place. We went to different to cafés where they specialized in really good coffee; to bakeries that baked their own pastries in-house (this is not a trivial matter, especially nowadays); and all along, we kept looking for new flavors. I think we were trying to figure out New York and the flavors that shaped this incredible city.

We visited one very special bakery in Brooklyn, the Four & Twenty Blackbirds Bakery. This bakery sat its customers at communal tables, while the other side functioned as a counter that served pies (and only pies), and we ate our pies on "old lady" plates with silver forks. It was there that we found truly special flavors. I don't remember everything we had that day, but I'll never forget the red grapefruit pie, and the bakery's signature salty honey pie, made with Maldon salt.

A few years later—several diplomas later, and many, many pies later—while I was working as a pastry chef at the well-known Tel Aviv restaurant Pronto, my chef, David Frenkel, told me that in addition to all the desserts, he wanted me to make a different tart every day for the afternoon customers. This would be a tart du jour—not a menu tart—and it could be any tart I wanted. And that's what I did, making a different tart every day to suit my mood: chocolate, pistachio, lemon meringue, and a caramelized walnut and almond cream tart (don't worry, I've got that one covered here as well; see page 223), which would become a regular fixture of our afternoon service for a long time, until it was replaced by the salty honey tart.

The first time I made a version of the salty honey tart, based on the one I ate at the Brooklyn bakery, it was love at first bite: for the chef, for the sous chef, for the waiters—and most importantly, for our customers. "What is this tart?" the chef asked excitedly. "Let's make this part of the regular menu!" It took me a few weeks, some fine tuning, and a few tests, and I came up with Pronto's salted honey tart. Thin slices of tart on a bed of espresso jelly, with a velvety honey crémeux (a kind of French custard) that was the perfect balance of sweet and salty, and rock bonbons made of almonds, cherry, and blond Dulcey chocolate. We served the dish with toasted wheat ice cream, and it was perfect. They continued to serve this dish at Pronto for years even after I was no longer working there, and even today they continue to serve a variation of it.

This tart is perfection, and what makes it so special is that it's not what you expect a tart to be—it's just so different from anything one imagines when ordering this dish, and even more. I've heard it compared to crack pie, but those who compare it to crack pie don't really understand this tart's unique flavors, which are so different. Yes, its texture is buttery and delightful, but it's the honey that makes it special. I love working with honey; unlike sugar, honey can change a pastry completely. In addition, there so many different types of honey—crystallized or smooth, honey cream, and even honey from a cotton flower—and each has a unique and interesting flavor. When combined with salt, honey becomes anything but what you expect, because salt and honey, surprisingly enough, complement each other. One other thing I love about this tart: it's simple enough that anyone can make it—not just pastry chefs!

So, a few years later, with knowledge from several culinary travels added to my arsenal, I came back from Japan with a suitcase full of utensils and raw materials. At one market, I purchased a paste made of black sesame and honey, when it hit me: This was the combination I was looking for! In the Levante (Middle Eastern countries), *halvah* (a sweetmeat made of sesame paste and nuts) is an everyday sweet that's sold in every store and market, but the Japanese use of sesame manages to surprise and challenge us every single time. Halvah, starchy, full of texture, and easy to chew, finds its match in its Japanese counterpart, which, surprisingly enough, has a jelly-like texture, although the flavors are very similar. In Israel we use halvah a lot, as do the Japanese their sesame paste. So I was surprised at how interested people were in my Honey, Black Sesame, and Sea Salt Tart, which I love. I think it's a truly unique dish, which manages to balance its flavors in an exceptional way.

A few years ago, 12 chefs who used to intern together at Noma, myself included, got together in the Netherlands to create and cook a special meal. Once it was created, we served it 6 times: lunch and dinner for 3 days. I served this tart as a part of my dessert offering, and all of the chefs went—how shall I put this mildly—nuts! It rarely happens that after a having an entire tasting menu for dinner, the dish that's most talked about is the dessert! However, I'm proud to say that, thanks to its unique look, which is a bit misleading because people assume it's a chocolate pie, and its extraordinary flavors, my dessert received the greatest accolades.

So here it is: my Honey, Black Sesame, and Sea Salt Tart—a Middle Eastern variation that's deceptively simple and completes every meal with a bang.

HONEY, BLACK SESAME, AND SEA SALT TART

Makes one 24-cm (9.5-in) tart pan

-

For the crust

2 ½ cups (350 grams) all-purpose flour

1 Tbs sugar

1 tsp sea salt

1 cup (220 grams) cold butter, cut into cubes

¼ Tbs vinegar mixed in 1 cup of cold water

-

For the filling

½ cup (110 grams) melted butter

1 cup minus 2 Tbs (180 grams) sugar

1 Tbs cornstarch

½ tsp sea salt

1 Tbs vanilla extract

⅓ cup (100 grams) honey

5 ¼ Tbs (80 grams) black sesame paste

3 eggs

½ cup (120 grams) heavy cream

2 Tbs vinegar

1–2 Tbs sea salt, for sprinkling

1. **Prepare the crust:** Place the flour, salt, sugar, and butter in the bowl of a stand mixer fitted with the paddle attachment, and mix to a texture resembling coarse meal.

2. Pour the vinegar-water slowly and while mixing continuously, just until the dough comes together. You may not need to use all of the water.

3. Roll into a ball, flatten to a disc, and cover in plastic wrap. Refrigerate for at least 1 hour.

4. Place the dough between two sheets of parchment paper and roll into a circle 5 mm (0.2 in) thick, 26-cm (10-in) in diameter. Transfer to the tart pan and press to the bottom and sides of the pan. Place in the freezer until ready to use.

5. Preheat the oven to 180 °C (350 °F).

6. **Prepare the filling:** Place the melted butter in a bowl and add the sugar, cornstarch, salt, vanilla, honey, and black sesame paste, and beat well with a whisk.

7. Add the eggs, one at a time, beating each egg until it's incorporated.

8. Add the heavy cream and vinegar and mix well.

9. Pour over the frozen crust and bake for 30–40 minutes, until the filling is set and golden.

10. Sprinkle sea salt on top and cool to room temperature.

TART DU JOUR: CARAMELIZED WALNUT AND ALMOND CREAM TART

As I've mentioned before, at Pronto (a famous Italian bistro in Tel Aviv) I had the pleasure of working with Chef David Frenkel, who loves and appreciates the art of pastry. David is a perfectionist and has a great appreciation for the precision required by pastry. When I started working at Pronto, David decided that he wanted to have a different tart each day, giving me ***carte blanche*** to make whichever tarts I wanted.

One day I made a caramelized nut and almond cream tart, which was based on a tart I had learned to make during my culinary studies in New York. That day, one of the restaurant partners was there, and after tasting the tart he said, "You have to make this every day!" So I began making this tart every day and it became "the tart" at Pronto. In fact, when a culinary magazine in Israel wrote an article about our dessert menu, they chose my tart to be on the cover of the magazine, so you can imagine how proud I am of this beautiful tart. You can make this tart with different nuts and it's always perfect!

Makes 1 20–24-cm (8–10-in) tart pan

–

For the crust

- 1/3 cup (40 grams) powdered sugar
- 6 Tbs (85 grams) butter, softened
- 1 egg at room temperature
- 1 cup + 1 Tbs (150 grams) all-purpose flour
- A pinch of baking powder

–

For the almond cream

- 14 Tbs (200 grams) butter, softened
- 1 cup (200 grams) sugar
- Seeds scraped from 1/4 vanilla pod
- 2 eggs at room temperature
- 2 cups (200 grams) almond meal
- 2 Tbs (20 grams) cornstarch

–

For the caramel walnut filling

- 1/3 cup + 1 Tbs (100 ml) heavy cream
- 1/3 cup + 1 Tbs (100 ml) milk
- 3/4 cup (150 grams) sugar
- A pinch of salt
- 1 Tbs corn syrup or honey
- 1 1/2 cups (150 grams) walnuts, chopped

→

1. **Prepare the caramel walnut filling:** Place the heavy cream and milk in a small pot over medium heat and bring to a gentle simmer. Set aside.

2. Place the sugar in an even layer in a heavy-bottomed pan. Heat over a low-medium heat until the sugar begins to melt. Add a pinch of salt and cook until the sugar turns to an amber caramel. Carefully add the corn syrup (or honey) and the warm cream to the caramel while stirring continuously, until it becomes a smooth caramel sauce.

3. Add the chopped walnuts and cook to a sauce the consistency of pancake batter. Cool. When ready to use, the cooled filling should have the consistency of a thick cream.

4. **Prepare the crust:** Place the powdered sugar and butter in the bowl of a stand mixer fitted with the paddle attachment and mix to a pale and fluffy cream. Add the egg and mix well. Add the flour and baking powder, and mix until just the dough comes together.

5. Roll into a ball, flatten to a disc, and cover in plastic wrap. Refrigerate for 1 hour.

6. **Prepare the almond cream:** Place the butter, sugar, and vanilla in the bowl of a stand mixer fitted with the paddle attachment, and mix to a pale and fluffy cream. Add the egg and mix well. Add the almond meal and cornstarch.

7. **Assemble the tart:** Preheat the oven to 180 °C (350 °F). Roll the dough out on lightly floured parchment paper to a 3-mm (0.1-in)-thick circle. Transfer to the tart pan and press to the bottom and sides of the pan. Freeze for 15 minutes.

8. Pour the caramel walnut filling on the frozen crust, and smooth to an even layer. Spread a layer of the almond cream on top, that touches the end of the pie pan. Smooth to an even layer.

9. Bake for 40 minutes, until the top of the tart is a deep shade of golden brown. Let cool completely.

A Classic French Pastry

When it comes to French pastries, cannelés de Bordeaux are a classic, and I have an ancient, long-lasting love affair with this pastry. I think it was my mom who first introduced me to cannelés; she would bring treats from the Brasserie (a well-known Tel Aviv restaurant), while I was hard at work at my restaurant, 6 days a week, 15 hours on my feet. I would come home and she would pamper me with two cannelés from the Brasserie. Cannelés de Bordeaux are considered a delicacy, and anyone who's tasted this wonder in France always ends up wanting more.

I'm not completely certain regarding when I began making cannelés, but it could have been while I was working as a pastry cook at Raphael (a famous restaurant in Tel Aviv). In those days Chef Rafi Cohen wanted to add cannelés to the dessert menu in some way (today I'm not even sure how he wanted to include them; perhaps as a petit four or perhaps as part of the breakfast menu in the new restaurant he wanted to open). Anyway, he was the only chef I remember who specifically asked me to make cannelés.

The cannelé is a bakery pastry, not a restaurant dessert, and that might be the reason why cannelés were virtually unknown in Israel until about eight years ago.

Years later, I became friends with Maya Marom, the talented person behind a well-known and beloved Israeli blog called *Bazek Alim* ("Violent Dough") (which is a play on words for the Hebrew name for puff pastry). Maya and I had real copper cannelé molds that we'd bought in Paris and never used, because, well, they're gorgeous, especially when they're new. Also, we were scared to use them. So we planned a joint baking day, and decided that on that day, we would "season" our copper molds. This is something that you need to do to the molds, using beeswax and butter (*see explanation on page 228*) before using them. Then we decided to bake our first cannelés in the copper molds, rather than in stainless steel or silicone molds.

Why are the copper molds better for cannelés? Because copper, which used to be used exclusively in kitchens, is one of the most evenly-conductive metals. So why is it used less today? Probably because it's more expensive than the soft, lighter metals, which are also simpler to clean. But when you look at the result, there's no comparison. Oh, and of course, the result is beautiful.

Let's talk for a moment about the story behind this pastry, because, like all beautiful things, it also has a story. So, we already know it originates from Bordeaux, France, but why and how? Bordeaux, as many know, has lots of vineyards and wineries, so they make wine there. In the past, they used to clarify the wine by using a method from the world of cooking called "consommé," a method that's used in clarifying soup. The process of making consommé requires using egg whites, which left the good people of Bordeaux with a lot of egg yolks, and they thought to themselves, "What will we do with them?"

So they invented this ingenious pastry, which has the aroma of beeswax, giving it a honey aroma without actually containing honey. The batter is as simple to make as pancake batter, with vanilla and rum flavors. The pastry itself is baked for a very long time; but when you look at this pastry and see just how small it is, the thought of baking it so long makes you pause. And yet, cannelés are indeed baked on a medium-hot setting for several hours. This long and hot baking—when combined with all the elements and the effect of the copper molds, of course—is what gives cannelés their unique texture and structure: a very dark, cracked, caramelized, hard shell, and an inside that's almost as soft as pudding.

Whenever I'm asked to describe the flavor of cannelés, I tell the person asking me that they have to try it for themselves, because there are certain things that have to be experienced—and words can never accurately describe this experience. Believe me, there's nothing quite like watching a person trying their first cannelé!

CANNELÉS DE BORDEAUX*

Although cannelés are best when made in copper molds, they can also be made in stainless steel molds and even silicone. The recipe is incredibly simple and insanely delicious, so it seems right to share it with you here.

Makes 10 cannelés

-

- 2 cups (480 ml) milk
- 2 Tbs (25 grams) melted butter
- 1 ½ cups (300 grams) sugar
- ¾ cup (100 grams) all-purpose flour
- ½ tsp salt
- 2 egg yolks
- 1 tsp vanilla extract or seeds scraped from 1 vanilla pod
- 1 Tbs chocolate liqueur (or any other liqueur of your choice)

Seasoning Copper Molds

Cannelés are traditionally baked in copper molds, which are largely responsible for the wonderful, crisp, caramelized exterior shell. Before we begin with the cannelés, the copper molds need to be "seasoned" in advance.

1. Gently wash the molds with soap and water, and dry thoroughly with a towel. Do not air dry as copper tends to oxidize quickly.

2. Melt ½ cup (50 grams) butter with ½ cup (50 grams) beeswax in a small pot.

3. Using a small brush, grease the copper molds, thoroughly.

4. Preheat the oven to 180 °C (350 °F). Place the greased molds in the oven and bake empty for 1 ½-2 hours. Pour out any residual grease and cool. The copper molds are now ready for use.

Preparing the Cannelés

1. Place 1 cup of milk and the butter in a small pot and bring to a gentle simmer, stirring occasionally.

2. Place the remaining milk and the sugar in a bowl and mix. Add the flour, salt and yolks, and whisk to a smooth batter. Pour the simmering milk mixture into the bowl slowly and while mixing continuously. Add the vanilla and liqueur and mix well.

3. Transfer the runny batter to an airtight container and refrigerate overnight or at least 8 hours.

→

4. Grease the cannelé molds with the melted butter and place in the freezer at least 30 minutes before baking (this will prevent the batter from sticking to the molds).

5. Preheat the oven to 180 °C (350 °F) and line a baking tray with parchment paper.

6. Place the greased molds on the tray and pour the batter, leaving a 5-mm (0.2-in) space from the top.

7. Bake for 1 ½–2 hours.

8. After 1½ hours, check one cannelé for doneness; the sides should be crispy and a deep dark brown color. If needed, bake a further 30 minutes.

9. Flip the cannelés immediately on a cooling rack and let cool for 30 minutes, during which time the caramel exterior will harden and become crisp.

*This recipe was created in collaboration with Chef Maya Marom

2020 was a year that very few of us will ever forget. It was the year we all stayed home (to save lives), practiced social distancing, and spent more time with our families than ever before. These recipes were the result of that time at home, when we couldn't rely on having access to all the necessary ingredients—sometimes not even the staple ones, like eggs and yeast—and they will remain with me as reminders of a very different world.

Love in the Time of Corona

I have two really vivid memories of pita as a child: One was making a pita pizza, which is essentially a pita sliced in half, covered with ketchup and cheese, then shoved into the toaster oven until the pita becomes crispy and the cheese melts. You can try to make it a bit fancier by adding spices, but we never did. Another memory is the classic pita with hummus. Like most children in Israel, I remember getting half a pita bread filled with hummus and slivers of pickles (in brine; in Israel very few kids will eat a dill pickle), which we would get either in class parties or on Lag Ba'Omer (a holiday that used to be celebrated with huge bonfires). I remember that we had this "discotheque" in Ra'anana (the town where I grew up) when we were in the fourth to sixth grades, and we'd go to the Youth House and dance and then we'd buy a pita with hummus and a pickle or a pita with chocolate spread for 10 shekels (today that's a little over $2). Yup, pita with chocolate spread or hummus was such a default for us as kids! Years later, while living in New York, I was doing my shopping and I found my childhood pitas in the form of "pita chips," while my hummus was now "hummus dip." Wow—what an upgrade!

Throughout my career, I've had the opportunity to make all kinds of flat breads, but I never got to fully master the pita bread. At Raphael, I used to make focaccias and everyone loved them. But most of the restaurants where I worked served either European or fusion cuisine, so flat bread was mostly something we made for the staff meals.

When I studied bread baking in New York, we had a section on flat bread that also touched on the ethnic roots of flat bread. Flat bread, we know, is deeply rooted in human history, including in our own Middle Eastern history of pita (with its various iterations). Other examples include naan, chapati, tortillas, and all sorts of flat breads from Africa and India that are integral to our everyday lives and to Western cuisine.

Just before Israeli Independence Day (Yom Ha'atzmaut), in the middle of the COVID-19 crisis, I was asked to come up with a recipe for pita (in Israel, Independence Day is celebrated with barbecues, salads, hummus, and enormous amounts of pita, even before you start eating any meat). I agreed, and reached out to my brother's friend in Australia, Yariv "Pitot," who makes pitas, of course. Yariv, however, couldn't help me, because he'd never made pitas at home—only in his bakery with the big stone oven. My answer to him was "challenge accepted" and I began to look at different recipes.

In the end I settled on a simple recipe, one that's also used for making bialy; interestingly enough, even though bialy is a very Eastern European Jewish bread, very few Israelis have any idea of what a bialy is! So I made bialy, and then, from the same dough, I made pitas, which I cooked on a pan on the stovetop (not inside the oven), since the pan behaves like a stone oven. The pitas came out perfect; I sent some to my mom and she loved them too and with good reason: These pitas are really tasty and rich with turmeric. Unlike a regular pita, which you can stuff (like the famous stuffed pitas of Chef Eyal Shani at Miznon in New York), they're flat and more like tortillas, and can be rolled up.

PITA BREAD

Makes 12 pitas

-

6 cups (840 grams) all-purpose flour or bread flour

3 tsp salt

1 ½ tsp (6 grams) active dry yeast

½ tsp ground turmeric

2 cups + 2 ½ Tbs (520 ml) water

Flour, for dusting

1. **The day before:** Place the flour, salt, yeast, turmeric, and water in the bowl of a stand mixer fitted with the dough hook. Mix on a low speed until the dough comes together. Increase the speed slightly and knead for 5 minutes, until you have a soft, smooth dough.

2. Transfer the dough to a greased bowl, shape into a ball, cover, and refrigerate overnight.

3. **The next day:** Divide the dough into 12 equal pieces, each weighing about 4.2 oz (120 grams), and roll into balls.

4. Line 2 baking trays with parchment paper and lightly flour. Place 6 balls on each tray, cover with a towel, and let rise at room temperature for 40 minutes.

5. Roll 2–3 balls on a lightly floured worksurface and flatten into circles, about 5 mm (0.2 in) thick.

6. Warm a cast iron skillet over medium-high heat. When the skillet is sizzling hot, place one pita on the skillet and fry for 2-3 minutes on each side. Place on a wire rack to cool and cover with a clean towel.

7. Repeat this with the remaining pitas, rolling and frying 2-3 balls at a time.

Eat immediately, as the pitas are best immediately after baking.

A Baker's Tip

Unlike regular bread, pitas should be packed immediately after being taken out of the oven. I know this because I once took a Latvian friend to the *shuk* (market) and told her to wait until the pita she'd bought cooled—but then I found out that packing the pitas while still hot—straight from the oven—on purpose is what keeps the pita soft, unlike any other kind of bread.

EGGLESS CHALLAH

This recipe was created when, for a period of time, it became impossible to get eggs in Israel. I think every country must have found itself in one shortage or another during the COVID-19 crisis, but in Israel, the first major shortage was eggs. A few weeks into the crisis, with everyone baking as a result of too much spare time, the shortage switched to yeast, then flour became scarce, vanilla extract, and so on.

Rising to the challenge of an eggless pantry, I decided to come up with a solution for recipes without eggs, especially challah, since most of my challahs call for eggs. The challah I came up with isn't vegan, since, although it doesn't contain eggs, it does include dairy. Creating the eggless challah took me quite a while, and there were several dramatic setbacks, but once I figured out a solution, this challah quickly became my favorite one. This is the softest challah ever; it's like a cloud in a loaf of challah.

→

→

Makes 1 eggless challah

-

For the dough

2 1/2 cups (350 grams) all-purpose flour or bread flour

1 tsp (4 grams) active dry yeast or 1 1/4 Tbs (10 grams) fresh yeast

3 1/2 Tbs (40 grams) sugar

3/4 tsp salt

1 cup minus 1 1/2 Tbs (220 ml) whole milk

4 Tbs (55 grams) butter, softened

-

For the glaze

2 Tbs date molasses

1/2 tsp water

Pearl sugar or sesame seeds

1. Place the flour, yeast, sugar, salt, and milk in the bowl of a stand mixer fitted with the dough hook. Mix on a low speed until the dough comes together. Increase the speed slightly and knead for 5 minutes, until you have a soft, smooth dough.

2. Add the butter and knead until it's fully incorporated into the dough.

3. Shape the dough into a ball, transfer to a greased bowl, cover with a towel or a loose plastic wrap and let rise for 30 minutes, until it doubles in volume.

4. Punch down the dough, cover, and let rise for another 30 minutes.

5. Butter and line a loaf pan with parchment paper.

6. Place the dough on a lightly floured surface and divide into 3 or 4 equal balls (for either a 3- or a 4-strand challah). Roll each ball into a strand 35-40 cm (13-15 in) long. I like my strands plumper in the center and thinner on the ends. Cover and let rest for 10 minutes.

7. Roll the strands and braid the challah (*see image on page 29 for instructions for braiding a 4-strand challah; a 3-strand challah is braided like a regular braid*). Carefully transfer to the baking pan.

8. **Prepare the glaze:** Mix the date molasses with the water and brush the challah with a thin coat. Let rise uncovered at room temperature for 1–1½ hours, until it doubles in volume.

9. Preheat the oven to 180 °C (350 °F).

10. Brush the challah with another thin coat of the glaze and sprinkle pearl sugar or sesame seeds on top.

11. Bake for 25–30 minutes, until the challah is a deep, even shade of golden brown. Cool on a rack.

Section 8

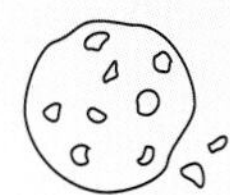

For No Special Reason

Everyday Baking

If you're like me, you probably get the urge to bake something for no special reason. These everyday recipes are easy to make and perfect for busy days. And the result? Well, let's just say you shouldn't expect many leftovers.

KREMUGIT COOKIE

In Israel there's a brand of cookie made by Osem (a huge snack manufacturer) called *Kremugit*—which means creme cookie. This cookie is made from a simple dough and filled with chocolate cream, and it is the best and tastiest cookie in the world. You can get it in all sorts of flavors: chocolate-banana, lemon, and more. The classic version is a vanilla cookie filled with chocolate cream or with nut-flavored cream, and as a child I loved these cookies.

A few months ago, my column editor at *Hashulchan* Magazine asked me for a recipe for kremugit, but her request caught me by surprise. I just couldn't remember what these cookies were; her request was very much a "blast from the past" for me. I decided to add kremugit cookies to my column wish list, and told her that I would tackle them at some point. And then our lives were transformed by the COVID-19 outbreak; I found myself with a lot of time on my hands, so I opened the wish list of all the recipes I never had a chance to make, and I decided to make kremugit cookies.

Despite the cookie's simplicity, it wasn't that easy to come up with a recipe in the beginning. This was not your classic sugar cookie dough: I added cinnamon and a bit of salt, and then I filled the cookies with milk chocolate. When they were ready, I took the cookies out of the oven and opened one up to see how it looked on the inside. I gave one, fresh from the oven, to Uri (my significant other), who was working from home at the time (like the rest of the world), and he asked me, "What is this?" "Don't you remember kremugit?" I answered him, and he replied, "I know kremugit, but I've never tasted anything like this."

So I tasted the cookie myself and I realized he was right! It was like no other cookie I'd ever tasted. I dedicated the recipe to my editor, and it's one of my most successful recipes so far, with people making it with their kids at home. The cookie keeps really well, and it's just a perfect cookie for our time, a more sophisticated kremugit that reminds us of our childhood and a simpler time.

→

→

Makes 20 cookies

–

1 cup (225 grams) butter at room temperature

¼ cup + 2 Tbs (75 grams) white sugar

⅓ cup (85 grams) light brown cane sugar

½ Tbs honey

2 ½ cups minus 1 Tbs (340 grams) all-purpose flour or pastry flour

¾ tsp baking soda

¾ tsp ground cinnamon

½ tsp salt

7 oz (200 grams) milk chocolate chips

1. Place the butter, sugars, and honey in the bowl of a stand mixer fitted with the paddle attachment and beat to a pale and fluffy mixture.

2. Place the flour, baking soda, cinnamon, and salt in a bowl and mix well. Add to the butter mixture slowly and while mixing on a low speed for several minutes, to a crumbly dough. Pinch a piece of the dough and press; if the dough comes together, transfer to a clean bowl, cover with plastic wrap, and refrigerate for 1 hour.

3. Divide the dough into 20 balls, each weighing about 1.4 oz (40 grams).

4. Cut each ball in half and roll each piece into a flat disc. Place 4–5 chocolate chips on one disc and cover with the remaining disc. Press to seal the edges and reshape to a circle. Repeat this with the remaining dough and chocolate chips. Place the cookies on a tray lined with parchment paper, leaving a 4-cm (1.5-in) gap between them, and refrigerate for 30 minutes.

5. Preheat the oven to 180 °C (350 °F).

6. Bake for 12 minutes, until golden. Let cool for 10 minutes before serving.

LEMON POPPY SEED CAKE

Around Rosh Hashanah (the Jewish New Year) I had an idea for a cake that I wanted to make using leftover lemon juice and poppy seed. I mixed the two together into a pound cake, made two cakes, and brought one over to my mom. We brought the other one to Uri's parents. When I handed them the cake, I apologized in advance for bringing something that I'd never tried before, and then apologized again in case it wasn't good.

Uri's parents usually like to have a dairy dish on Saturday morning, so after his father came back from morning prayers, everyone took a piece of the cake, and then, there was silence around the table. They all took another piece. Uri's father turned to me and said, "This is the first time I've had poppy seed in a cake and liked it!" After tasting the cake I knew what he meant; I usually don't like poppy seed as a filling, only as a topping, and only when it's crunchy. But that's why I wanted to make this cake the way I did—a lemon cake dotted with spots. Everyone around the table loved the cake and told me I should start selling it, but first, I called my mom and told her she had to try the cake I'd brought over. Of course, she loved it too. The thing is, this cake is just perfect—not too tart and not too sweet—just perfect.

→

Makes 1 Bundt cake pan

-

For the cake

A little over 1/3 cup (50 grams) poppy seeds

1/3 cup + 1 Tbs (100 ml) freshly squeezed lemon juice

14 Tbs (200 grams) butter, at room temperature

1 1/2 cups (300 grams) sugar

1/2 tsp salt

4 eggs

1 brick cream cheese or about 1 cup (250 grams) mascarpone cheese

3 cups (420 grams) all-purpose flour

2 1/2 tsp (10 grams) baking powder

7 oz (200 grams) sour cream

-

For the icing

3 1/2 Tbs (50 ml) freshly squeezed lemon juice

1 1/2 cups (200 grams) powdered sugar

1/4 cup (30 grams) poppy seeds

1. Place the poppy seeds and lemon juice in a bowl and let sit for 30 minutes.

2. Preheat the oven to 180 °C (350 °F) and butter the cake pan.

3. Place the butter and sugar in the bowl of a stand mixer fitted with the paddle attachment and beat until light and fluffy.

4. Add the poppy seeds and lemon juice and beat until incorporated.

5. Add the eggs, one at a time, and beat after each addition until the egg is fully incorporated.

6. Add the cream cheese (or mascarpone), flour, baking powder, and sour cream and mix until just combined (avoid overmixing).

7. Pour the batter into the cake pan and smooth the top with a spatula.

8. Bake for 30–40 minutes, until a toothpick inserted in the center comes out clean. Let the cake cool in the pan for about 10 minutes before releasing it and transferring to a wire rack.

9. **Prepare the icing:** Mix the powdered sugar and lemon juice to a smooth paste. Place parchment paper under the wire rack and pour the icing over the cake.

10. Sprinkle poppy seeds and let the icing set for 10 minutes.

PEACH COBBLER IN A SKILLET

I like to use spice sugar or pumpkin spice (*see recipe on page 106*) in this recipe, and of course, you can make this cobbler with any fruit that's in season.

Makes one 20-cm (8-in) skillet

-

For greasing the skillet

2 Tbs (30 grams) melted butter

2 Tbs sugar

-

For the batter

3 Tbs (45 grams) melted butter

2 large eggs

¾ cup (150 grams) sugar

1 tsp vanilla extract

1 ¼ cup (180 grams) all-purpose flour

1 ½ tsp baking powder

½ tsp salt

1 cup (230 ml) milk

-

For the fruit

2 Tbs (25 grams) light brown cane sugar

1 ½ Tbs (7 grams) cornstarch

16 oz (450 grams) peaches, quartered

Freshly squeezed juice from ½ lemon

A pinch of salt

-

For the spiced sugar (alternatively, use cinnamon or vanilla sugar)

3 Tbs pumpkin spice (*see recipe on page 106*)

2 Tbs light brown sugar

¼ tsp ground black pepper

1 tsp vanilla sugar

-

Serve with

Whipped cream, crème fraîche, or ice cream

1. **Prepare the spiced sugar:** Place all the ingredients in a bowl and mix well. Transfer to a small jar and set aside.

2. **Prepare the fruit:** Place the sugar and cornstarch in a bowl and mix well. Add the sliced fruit, lemon juice, and salt, and mix well until the fruit is fully coated. Set aside.

3. **Prepare the skillet:** Preheat the oven to 180 °C (350 °F). Grease a cast-iron skillet with the melted butter and sprinkle 2 tablespoons of sugar to coat.

4. **Prepare the batter:** Place the eggs, sugar, melted butter, and vanilla extract in the bowl of a stand mixer fitted with the paddle attachment and mix to a pale and fluffy cream.

5. Place the flour, baking powder, and salt in a separate bowl and mix well.

→

6. Add several tablespoons of the flour mixture to the mixer and mix well. Add several tablespoons of milk and mix well. Continue with the remaining flour mixture and milk, alternating between them, until just combined (don't overmix).

7. Pour the mixture into the skillet and sprinkle the spiced sugar.

8. Spread the sliced fruit on top evenly and bake for 45–60 minutes, until the fruit is bubbling and the cobbler is golden.

9. Cool for 10 minutes before serving with whipped cream, crème fraîche, or your favorite ice cream.

LE CREUSET

My Love Affair with Olive Oil

I love baking with olive oil; nowadays, it's the only oil I use at home aside from butter (although I use oil sprays for my trays), and if you ever see oil as an ingredient in my recipes, it's always olive oil. I switched to olive oil exclusively when I began to use really high-quality olive oil and I learned where to buy it (not all olive oil is good quality, so be sure to find one that is). My olive oil vendor asked if I knew how to truly identify a good-quality olive oil, and to help me, he gave me an olive oil tasting, so that I could really feel the difference between the different oils. For the first time, I was able to taste the difference, the sharpness, the herbaceous (fruity, grassy, peppery) notes, and all sorts of other flavors that I never knew existed in olive oil. Right then I knew I was going to stick with this vendor for all of my olive oil, because he's truly a professional.

The same vendor told me that he used olive oil for everything, including baking, and now I've also switched to olive oil for everything—even for challah and for my babka cakes! I also decided to use olive oil exclusively because it's locally made—we have so many wonderful types of olives to choose from and, as a result, a wide selection of excellent oils. Now a lot of people think that olive oil is bitter and has a very dominant flavor, but there are actually a lot of different olives that produce oil that's delicate and subtle and perfect for baking and cooking, and then there are the varieties that are really full-bodied and meant to stand out and to add flavor and seasoning.

A few months ago I was interviewed for a podcast called *Talking Isn't Fattening* and was asked about baking with olive oil, which gave me a chance to talk about this switch to using olive oil instead of vegetable or corn oil. Cold pressed, unrefined olive oil is one of the most natural and healthy oils there are, and it's also really tasty. And I brought up a point I make in all my workshops: Whereas in the past we used to use cooking wine, today we use the wine we like to drink in our cooking, and the same goes for our oil. Why should I bake with a clear, highly-processed, refined oil instead of something that's natural and tastes good on its own? An oil that has a wonderful color and smell and that only adds to and enriches my pastry?

CHOCOLATE & PISTACHIO BROWNIES IN A SKILLET

After I began to use olive oil exclusively, I thought, why not make a dessert with olive oil, if it works so well in other dishes? I decided to combine olive oil and chocolate, two ingredients that are each quite dominant and still work well together. I made my brownies without any butter (only olive oil) and added pistachios, which I also love. The result is a dessert that's completely parve (because there's no dairy or milk products in it) so there's no limitation on when you can eat it (if you keep kosher or if you're lactose-intolerant). The taste is very rich and the texture is wonderful. And if you want to treat yourself, add ice cream on top and eat with a spoon straight from the skillet.

Makes one 20-cm (8-in) skillet or one 8-in (20-cm) square brownie pan

-

½ cup + 1 Tbs (125 grams) extra virgin olive oil

1 cup (150 grams) dark chocolate with a minimum of 60% cocoa solids, chopped

⅓ cup (50 grams) milk chocolate, chopped

1 espresso shot or 1 Tbs instant coffee granules

1 ¼ cups (250 grams) sugar

2 large eggs

1¼ cups (165 grams) cake flour

1 tsp (5 grams) baking powder

1 tsp salt

3 Tbs pistachio paste (available online and in specialty shops)

A handful of shelled pistachios

1. Preheat the oven to 170 °C (340 °F) and lightly grease a cast-iron skillet or brownie baking pan (if you're baking in a pan, you'll also need to line it with parchment paper).

2. Place the olive oil and chocolates in a heat-proof bowl over a saucepan of simmering water (bain-marie) and heat, stirring occasionally, until melted. Add the espresso shot (or instant coffee granules), mix, and set aside.

3. Place the sugar and eggs in the bowl of a stand mixer fitted with the paddle attachment and mix until pale and fluffy.

4. Reduce the speed and pour the melted chocolate mixture while mixing continuously.

5. Add the flour and baking powder, and mix just until the mixture is smooth with no lumps.

6. Pour the batter into the skillet or brownie pan and smooth the top with a spatula.

7. Pour the pistachio cream into a piping bag and drizzle lines over the brownie batter. Using a toothpick, draw over the lines to create swirls. Sprinkle the shelled pistachios.

8. If you prefer your brownies on the fudgier side, bake for 35 minutes, if on the drier side, bake for a further 10 minutes.

9. Cool completely in the skillet or pan.

THE MOST DELICIOUS CHOCOLATE CHIP COOKIES IN THE WORLD

While studying in New York, in the middle of a grueling, Sisyphean day of baking in the bread bakery, I noticed that our chef, Brynne Thomas, was making cookies. The cookies were unusually dark, so I waited to see how they would turn out. When they came out of the oven, the cookies filled the bakery with this incredible aroma. "These are my favorite chocolate chip cookies, and 80 percent of their flour is buckwheat flour," said Brynne, as she dipped the cookies into milk and waited until they became even softer. These cookies were the best thing that happened to me that week; I asked Brynne, who would become a good friend, for the recipe, and she shared it with me gladly. I've made them countless times, for countless occasions, with 100 percent white flour, with buckwheat flour, and even with spelt flour.

I've made these cookies with chocolate chips and I've also put in all the sweet leftovers I had in the pantry and called them "leftover cookies." I've also shared this recipe on my blog (after being called out for taking too long to post it), and anyone who tries these cookies once gets instantly addicted. The thing about chocolate chip cookies is that, while their recipes are quite simple, they don't always come out the way you want them to. But this recipe will never let you down. So go into the kitchen and make some, and let's see how you feel about them in about 30 minutes.

Makes 18-22 cookies

-

1 3/4 cups (380 grams) light brown sugar

1 cup (225 grams) butter, at room temperature

1 tsp fine salt

2 eggs

1 tsp vanilla extract

3 cups (425) grams all-purpose flour

1/2 Tbs (4 grams) baking soda

2 1/4 cups (370 grams) dark chocolate with a minimum of 60% cocoa solids, chopped

Sea salt for sprinkling

1. Preheat the oven to 180 °C (375 °F) and line a baking tray with parchment paper.

2. Place the light brown sugar, butter, and salt in the bowl of a stand mixer fitted with the paddle attachment, and beat to a light and fluffy mixture.

3. Beat the eggs in, one at a time, mixing well after adding each one. Add the vanilla extract.

4. Add the flour, baking soda, and the chopped chocolate, and mix only until combined.

5. Using an ice cream scoop, scoop balls of the cookie dough and place on the baking tray, keeping them evenly spaced, as they will spread in the oven.

6. Sprinkle a few grains of sea salt on each cookie and bake for 14–17 minutes, until lightly brown on the edges and slightly soft in the center. I like my cookies soft in the center, so I bake them for 14 minutes, but if you prefer yours on the crunchier side, leave them for 17 minutes. Cool on a wire rack.

BUCKWHEAT CHOCOLATE CHIP COOKIES VARIATION

For a healthier version of these cookies, substitute the flour in the recipe with **⅔ cup (85 grams) all-purpose flour** and **2 ¾ cups (340 grams) buckwheat flour**.

SPELT FLOUR CHOCOLATE CHIP COOKIES VARIATION

If you want to reduce the amount of white flour in your cookies, substitute the flour in the recipe with **⅔ cup (85 grams) all-purpose flour** and **2 ¾ cups (340 grams) spelt flour**. Your kids will never know the difference and you'll love giving them these cookies.

Acknowledgements

To my mom, my guiding star on this planet, without whom some of my dreams could not come true, including this book, which I've been talking about for nearly a decade. My mom, who has always been there for me, supporting me; whether through her words, through her faith in me, always my tail wind. You, who brought me into the kitchen with love even as a child, encouraged me to try and to taste, encouraged me to open cookbooks and not to be afraid. So much of everything I've accomplished I owe to you.

To my grandmothers, who, to my regret, never had the chance to taste my pastries. To Grandma (Savta) Vicki; while writing this book, I understood even more how your approach to food and to its role as a central part of family life influenced me. To Grandma Pika (Rivka), whom my mom says I take after the most: I wish I could have learned to cook and bake with you in the kitchen. Writing this book has brought me closer to you both, and I hope you feel it, too, from above. To my Grandpa Gideon, who told me many years ago that I had a gift that I needed to develop into a profession, and who was, to his last day, my favorite client, who always loved chocolate, always finished every last bit from his plate, and always took pride in his pastry chef granddaughter.

To my brothers, Amit and Yoav, each of whom has been there and supported me in their own way, always. Your faith in my work and in my chosen path has always kept me strong. Thank you for always being there.

To Uri, my love, my partner. How can I find the words to describe just how you much you've supported me along the way? Your faith in my story, in my work, in my recipes and in my food, and your ability to keep reminding me to continue to dream, even when I get tired. You are my top taster, my sharpest critic, and most of all, you are my love. Thank you for all that you are.

To Chef Toni, your voice will always be there to guide me, in the good moments and in the worst ones. You will always be my mentor, my most esteemed and loved chef, and your voice is the one I hear that keeps telling me to stride forward.

To Brynne, who, for so long, has been more than just my chef, but also my beloved friend. From the moment I met you, you taught me that more than any great recipe in the world, the first thing a pastry chef needs is the instinct for baking. Thank you for placing a mirror before me that showed me what was there all along—I would have never found that part of me without you. Thank you for your knowledge and support, and most of all for your friendship.

I would also like to thank my followers and readers, both old and new, in Israel and throughout the world. Thanks to you, this book has finally come to be. Thank you for the love you show me every day, for loving the things you see and read, and for tasting my recipes. Thank you for being here.

Thank you to the amazing Anna, through whom I truly understood my story. Anna, who translated and edited my memories and stories in a way I never expected at my young age, so that the texts that emerged truly moved me, and to Karen for making sure the texts were perfect.

Thank you, Nomi, whose culinary editing, knowledge, and methodology made working through the recipes a true delight.

To Galia, Michal, Keren, and Noa, for the days of preparation, and for the long, fruitful photography sessions. Thank you to each of you for your creativity, style, thoughtfulness, and the ability to convey my story through the images. Thank you to Keren and Golan for making this work a reality, turning it into a stunning book.

And thank you to Ofer, whether near or far, who has been accompanying my dream of publishing this book for five years, and has fulfilled it in a way beyond my imagination.

Er sagt: „Entschuldigung“, und steht auf. Er geht wieder in die Toilette. Er schaut sich im Spiegel (mirror) an und denkt: „Ich sehe wie eine haarige Ratte aus.“ Er rasiert sein Gesicht. Er hat fast keinen Bart mehr. Dann versucht er wieder, seine Handflächen zu rasieren. Er versucht, alle Haare auf seinen Handflächen zu rasieren. Seine Hände sehen jetzt normal aus. Der Junge ist aber sauer und er schlägt auf das Waschbecken. Das Waschbecken zerbricht. Gerade dann kommt der Besitzer des Restaurants in die Toilette.

Er schreit den Jungen an: „Du wirst für die Reparatur des Waschbeckens bezahlen. Das kann man nicht mit Klebeband reparieren.“

Der Junge sagt: „Es tut mir Leid. Ich wollte das Waschbecken nicht zerbrechen.“ Er gibt dem Besitzer die $1000 Bargeld. Der Besitzer ist jetzt in guter Laune (good mood).

Der Junge geht wieder zu der Studentin und setzt sich. Er weint fast. Er **erklärt** der Frau alles. Er sagt ihr, dass er sie liebt, aber dass sie nur Männer mit Bart mag. Er **erklärt** ihr dann alles über den goldenen Schlüssel, das FBI und die Flasche. Sie hat Mitleid mit ihm (has sympathy for him) und versucht, ihn zu trösten (comfort). Sie umarmt ihn und küsst ihn. Sie sagt: „Du hast Recht. Ich mag Männer mit Bart. Aber ich mag dich auch. Ich habe jeden Mittwochabend frei. Willst du mit mir zu diesem Restaurant kommen? Ich kann bezahlen.“

Er lächelt und sagt: „Ja. Das wäre (would be) sehr schön."

Der Junge geht dann nach Hause. Er muss sich jeden Tag zweimal rasieren, aber endlich sind seine Handflächen und sein Gesicht wieder normal. Er versucht nicht mehr, sich schnell einen Bart wachsen zu lassen.

English meaning of words in bold type

Er hat keine Chance, mit der Frau zu gehen. = He has no chance to go out with the woman.
die Fabrik = the factory
die Flasche = the bottle
schmiert...ein = smears on (here), greases
einschmieren = to smear on (here) , to grease
erklärt = explains
erklären = to explain

Geschichte 28 - 2

Target words and phrases

Many of the target words and phrases in the previous stories are used in this last story.

Sie mochte nur Männer mit Bart

(Conversationl past)

Ein Junge hat eine Frau geliebt. Er war nur fünfzehn Jahre alt. Sie war Studentin an der Ohio State Universität. Die Frau war 19 Jahre alt. Sie **mochte** nur Männer mit Bart. Sie mochte keine Jungen. Der Junge hatte aber keinen Bart. Er ist die Straße entlang gegangen und hat hinunter auf den Gehsteig (sidewalk) geschaut. Er war unglücklich. **Er hatte keine Chance, mit der Frau zu gehen.**

Plötzlich hat er einen goldenen Schlüssel gesehen. Auf dem Schlüssel ist eine Adresse gestanden. Er hat gedacht: „Vielleicht geben sie mir eine Belohnung (a reward), wenn ich den Schlüssel zurückgebe." Er ist zur Adresse gegangen. Die Adresse war eine **Fabrik**. Die Fabrik **hieß** „ROGAIN." Der Junge ist zur Rezeption gegangen. Die Frau bei der Rezeption hat den Chef (boss) angerufen und hat ihm vom goldenen Schlüssel erzählt.

Der Chef ist gelaufen gekommen und hat den Jungen gefragt, wo er den Schlüssel gefunden hat. Der Junge hat gesagt, dass er den Schlüssel um die Ecke gefunden hat. Der Chef hat dem Jungen $1000 Bargeld (cash) gegeben und hat zu ihm gesagt, er soll mit niemandem über den Schlüssel reden. Der Junge ist sehr glücklich gewesen. Er ist aus der Fabrik gelaufen und hat vor Freude (joy) gelacht. Er ist um die Ecke gelaufen und ist gegen eine junge Frau gestoßen. Sie ist auf

ihren Hintern gefallen. Er **hat** sie **aufgehoben** und hat : „Entschuldigung“ gesagt.

Sie hat gesagt: „Ich bin OK. Warum läufst du um die Ecke? Das ist gefährlich (dangerous).“ Aber dann hat er wieder gelacht. Sie hat ihn komisch angeschaut und hat gesagt: „Warum lachst du? Ich bin auf den Boden gefallen und du lachst?“

Der Junge hat gesagt: „Entschuldigung, aber ich habe gerade $1000 Bargeld für einen kleinen goldenen Schlüssel bekommen.“

Sie hat gefragt: „Wer hat dir das Geld gegeben?“

„Der Chef von der ROGAIN **Fabrik** hat mir das Geld gegeben“, hat der Junge gesagt.

Die junge Frau hat gesagt: „Ich bin Reporterin an der Boston Globe-Zeitung. Bitte sage mir alles, was der Chef dir gesagt hat.“

Der Junge hat geantwortet: „Ich mag deine Zeitung, aber ich habe dem Chef versprochen (promised), dass ich meinen Mund halte.“

Dann hat die Frau gesagt: „Ich arbeite für die Zeitung, aber ich arbeite wirklich (really) für das FBI. Du kannst mir helfen. Was hat dir der Chef alles gesagt?“

Der Junge hat gesagt: „Der Chef hat mir nichts gesagt, aber die Frau bei der Rezeption hat mir gesagt, dass der Schlüssel für eine goldene Tür im Keller ist. Sie hat mir gesagt, dass sie dort neue Produkte erfinden (invent). Im Keller ist ein großes Labor (laboratory).“

Die FBI-Frau hat gesagt: „Es ist bald dunkel. Wir haben nicht viel Zeit. Wenn es dunkel wird, wechseln (change) sie die Wachen (the guards). Die Wachen sprechen für fünf Minuten. Wir können dann in den Keller kriechen.“

Sobald es dunkel war, sind sie in den Keller gekrochen. Sie haben die goldene Tür gefunden. Die FBI-Frau hatte einen High-Tech-Schlüssel. Sie hat die Tür aufgemacht. Sie haben das Labor betreten und haben sich umgeschaut. Niemand war im Labor. Sie haben sich umgeschaut und haben Flaschen (bottles) gefunden. Auf den Flaschen hat „Streng geheim“ (top secret) gestanden. Auf jeder Flasche hat auch „Achtung! Nur für Haarwachstumsexperimente (for hair growing experiments)“ gestanden. Die Frau hat gesagt: „Genau das suche ich.“ Sie hat eine **Flasche** genommen und hat gesagt: „Wir werden es im FBI-Labor analysieren.“

Während die Frau nicht zugeschaut hat, hat der Junge auch eine **Flasche** genommen und hat sie in seine Tasche gesteckt. Er hat gedacht: „Jetzt kann ich mir einen Bart wachsen lassen.“

Beide sind aus der Fabrik geschlichen (sneaked). Die Frau ist gleich zum FBI-Labor gefahren und der Junge ist nach Hause gegangen. Er war in seinem Badezimmer und **hat** sein Gesicht mit der grünen Flüssigkeit (fluid) **eingeschmiert** (smeared).

Am nächsten Tag ist er zur Uni (university) gegangen und hat die Studentin getroffen. Er hatte jetzt einen schwarzen Bart. Er hat mit ihr gesprochen und sie haben ein Restaurant betreten. Das Restaurant war neben einem Wal-Mart.

Die Studentin **mochte** den Jungen sehr, weil er so gut mit seinem Bart ausgesehen hat. Sie wusste nicht, dass er nur fünfzehn Jahre alt war. Aber dann gab es ein Problem. Der Junge hat gemerkt, dass Haar an seinen Handflächen (palms) angefangen hat zu wachsen. Er hat gesagt: „Entschuldigung. Ich muss meine Hände waschen.“ Er ist schnell weggegangen.

Er ist zum Wal-Mart gerannt und hat einen Rasierapparat gekauft. Er ist in die Toilette gegangen und hat

seine Handflächen rasiert. Der Besitzer des Wal-Markt ist in die Toilette gekommen und hat gesagt: „Sie sollen sich nicht in der Toilette rasieren." Der Junge ist dann zurückgegangen, hat wieder das Restaurant betreten und hat sich gesetzt.

Die Frau hat ihn angeschaut und hat gesagt: „Dein Bart ist sehr lang. Wie oft rasierst du dich?" Der Junge hat seinen Bart berührt (touched gently) und gemerkt, dass der Bart sehr lang war.

Er hat „Entschuldigung" gesagt und ist aufgestanden. Er ist wieder in die Toilette gegangen. Er hat sich im Spiegel (mirror) angeschaut und hat gedacht: „Ich sehe wie eine haarige Ratte aus." Er hat sein Gesicht rasiert. Er hatte fast keinen Bart mehr. Dann hat er wieder versucht, seine Handflächen zu rasieren. Er hat versucht, alle Haare auf seinen Handflächen zu rasieren. Seine Hände haben jetzt normal ausgesehen. Der Junge war aber sauer und hat auf das Waschbecken geschlagen. Das Waschbecken ist zerbrochen. Gerade dann ist der Besitzer des Restaurants in die Toilette gekommen.

Er hat den Jungen angeschrien: „Du wirst für die Reparatur des Waschbeckens bezahlen. Das kann man nicht mit Klebeband reparieren."

Der Junge hat gesagt: „Es tut mir Leid. Ich wollte das Waschbecken nicht zerbrechen.“ Er hat dem Besitzer die $1000 Bargeld gegeben. Der Besitzer war jetzt in guter Laune (good mood).

Der Junge ist wieder zur Studentin gegangen und hat sich gesetzt. Er hat fast geweint. Er **hat** der Frau alles **erklärt**. Er hat ihr gesagt, dass er sie liebt, aber dass sie nur Männer mit Bart mag. Er **hat** ihr dann alles über den goldenen Schlüssel, das FBI und die Flasche **erklärt**. Sie hatte Mitleid mit ihm (had sympathy for him) und hat versucht, ihn zu trösten (comfort). Sie hat ihn umarmt und geküsst. Sie hat gesagt: „Du hast Recht. Ich mag Männer mit Bart. Aber ich mag dich auch. Ich habe jeden Mittwochabend frei. Willst du mit mir zu diesem Restaurant kommen? Ich kann bezahlen.“

Er hat gelächelt und gesagt: „Ja. Das wäre (would be) sehr schön.“

Der Junge ist dann nach Hause gegangen. Er musste sich jeden Tag zweimal rasieren, aber endlich waren seine Handflächen und sein Gesicht wieder normal. Er hat nicht mehr versucht, sich schnell einen Bart wachsen zu lassen.

English meaning of words in bold type

mochte = liked   mögen = to like, to be fond of

Er hatte keine Chance, mit der Frau zu gehen. = He had no chance to go out with the woman.

die Fabrik = the factory

hieß = was called   heißen = to be called

hat…aufgehoben = picked up   aufheben = to pick up

die Flasche = the bottle

hat…eingeschmiert = smeared

schmiert...ein = smears on (here), greases

hat…erklärt = explained   erklären = to explain

Acknowledgements

I am indebted to several people who helped make this book possible. I'd like to thank my wife for her patience and encouragement as I was chasing my dream of teaching German. Her encouragement to begin publishing the stories was key to making this book a reality. I also want to thank Sabine Rankin for her proof-reading and invaluable German language insight. Thanks to Claudia Lawson for proofreading the third edition.

Jim Kramer, Bill Roys, Matt Blackwell, and Patrick Smallwood gave me frequent information systems support and guidance. Thanks to Elizabeth Vest. She gave her artistic talent and special effort to attractively illustrate each story.

Lastly, I'd like to thank my students in high school who read and "test drove" all the short stories. Not to be forgotten are my current adult students who "test drove" the three supplemental stories in the third edition.

Made in the USA
Columbia, SC
28 August 2020